Advan...

"*Scaling with Soul* isn't just a story about building a successful business—it's a captivating journey of adversity and triumph with themes of grit and grace that will resonate with anyone crafting their own success story."

**—HEATHER E. BURNS,
SERIAL SOCIAL ENTREPRENEUR**

"In her candid memoir, Gillenwater shares the remarkable story of her life-changing sale of her company as a bootstrapped entrepreneur. Packed with invaluable insights and hard-won lessons, *Scaling with Soul* is an absolute must-read for any aspiring founder."

**—MICHAEL BLEND, CO-FOUNDER, CEO
AND BOARD CHAIRMAN OF SYSTEM1**

"Filled with crazy backstories, emotion and valuable tips for any entrepreneur, *Scaling with Soul* is a revelation. Who knew a business book could be such a wild and rollicking ride?"

**—TINA DUONG,
FOUNDER OF IMPACTPRO TECH**

"In *Scaling with Soul*, Gillenwater delivers a raw and exciting tale of building a startup from scratch with transparency, honesty and integrity. It will have you on the edge of your seat."

—NOMIKI PETROLLA,
FOUNDER OF PDS LAB,
ENTREPRENEUR AND STARTUP MENTOR

"Diving into *Scaling With Soul* is like enjoying a gin and tonic on vacation: effervescent, fun, refreshing and gets the job done!"

—ERICA PARISI,
FOUNDER OF HIWIRE COSTUMES

How I Built
and Sold a
$25 Million
Tech Company
Without Being
an A**hole

Scaling
WITH
Soul

* Sharon K. Gillenwater *

LEGACY
launch pad
PUBLISHING

Copyright © 2024 by Sharon K. Gillenwater

All rights reserved.

No part of this book may be reproduced in any form or by any electronic or mechanical means, including information storage and retrieval systems, without written permission from the author, except for the use of brief quotations in a book review.

ISBN: 978-1-964377-00-1 (ebook)

ISBN: 978-1-964377-01-8 (paperback)

ISBN: 978-1-964377-02-5 (hardcover)

ISBN: 978-1-964377-03-2 (audiobook)

Front cover design by William Salit Design

Back cover design by One Graphica

Interior design layout by Noble Thread Designs

Although the publisher and the author have made every effort to ensure that the information in this book was correct at press time and while this publication is designed to provide accurate information in regard to the subject matter covered, the publisher and the author assume no responsibility for errors, inaccuracies, omissions, or any other inconsistencies herein and hereby disclaim any liability to any party for any loss, damage, or disruption caused by errors or omissions, whether such errors or omissions result from negligence, accident, or any other cause.

The publisher and the author do not make any guarantee or other promise as to any results that may be obtained from using the content of this book. You should never make any investment decision without first consulting with your own financial advisor and conducting your own research and due diligence. To the maximum extent permitted by law, the publisher and the author disclaim any and all liability in the event any information, commentary, analysis, opinions, advice and/or recommendations contained in this book prove to be inaccurate, incomplete or unreliable, or result in any investment or other losses.

To my mother, who inspired me.
To my husband, who believed in me.
To my sons, who motivated me.
To my mentors, who counseled me.
And to my friends, who put up with me.

Contents

Prologue: The Payoff

TWO LOUD CHIMES sounded through the airplane cabin, alerting the passengers and crew that our plane had reached 10,000 feet. Seconds later, the senior flight attendant cheerfully began her PA address, informing everyone that electronic devices were now approved for use. Then she invited us all to sit back, relax and enjoy the flight from Charlotte, North Carolina to San Francisco.

I felt anything but relaxed. Before the attendant could even finish the announcement, I'd grabbed my cell phone, enabled Wi-Fi and checked for messages.

Nothing.

My mind raced. Had something gone wrong? Was the closing delayed—again? Did the buyer back out at the last minute?

I was about to finalize the sale of my company, Boardroom Insiders, for $25 million. It was a life-changing amount of money. In fact, many at the company—my partner Lee, our shareholders and vested employees—stood to receive substantial payouts. New careers would be forged for our trusted employees as the buyer prepared to scale and expand Boardroom Insiders across the globe.

This moment would transform everything—my future, my dreams, my legacy.

No one would have predicted I'd ever get here—not even me. According to conventional wisdom, I wasn't the type of person to become a successful tech entrepreneur. My parents hadn't gone to college. We never sat around the dinner table talking about business. I had no interest in that world and knew nothing about it. Aside from a failed effort to sell painted flowerpots at the local flea market, I had no track record as an entrepreneur.

Though I lived smack-dab in the center of the entrepreneurial universe, I decidedly did not fit the typical Silicon Valley profile. I wasn't a Harvard or Stanford graduate. The education factories that churn out dealmakers, entrepreneurs and CEOs had passed me by. In fact, I'd accomplished almost nothing of note in my youth. I'd entered grad school at age 28 because I didn't know what else to do.

Even after grad school, I approached my career in the same haphazard and reactive fashion as I had when I was waiting tables in college: I worked for anyone who agreed to hire me. I couldn't articulate my skills and had no clue what I wanted to do, so I felt lucky to be offered anything.

I didn't come from a world where people were strategic and intentional about career decisions. The reality for most of my family was that there were few "careers." When someone needed money, they got a job. They weren't supposed to like it. I was well into my adulthood before I figured out there was another way.

Founding Boardroom Insiders was a tremendous leap of faith—faith that my life and work could have an impact that reached far beyond anything I'd previously thought possible. It represented a change in my worldview—breaking free of the mindset I'd grown up with, casting off the limiting beliefs that kept me from realizing that greater things were within my grasp

—that I not only deserved them but could *create* them, all on my own. And I built the business to mirror that ideal, with employee development as our ensign and outsize principles as our rudder. Over the years, the company had become my second home. The people there were more than just employees. They'd become like family.

For a moment, I regretted my decision to fly home at such a crucial time. But for the third time in as many days, the final transaction had been delayed. I'd been at our South Carolina office for two weeks, working on the sale around the clock. The lawyers, the deal team and the buyer all required a massive amount of paperwork. It didn't matter if I'd already sent the exact same information, in triplicate. Someone would request it again in a different format.

They had questions about every aspect of the business, down to the most minute details. I dutifully answered every single one, even if I sometimes wondered whether the buyer reviewed its own material. Of all the questions asked, my favorite was: "Who is Sharon Gillenwater and what is her role?"

I wanted to scream, "SHE'S THE FUCKING FOUNDER AND CEO!" But this CEO wanted her fucking money so I sucked it up and sent the requested information in a professional manner. But the truth is, I had been asking myself the very same question for years, before Boardroom Insiders came to be. Who was I, where did I fit in and what did I want to contribute?

I'd founded Boardroom Insiders and nurtured it for 14 years, working tirelessly to build and scale the business, even while so many people told me it wouldn't work. My partner, Lee, joined the company a couple of years into the journey. Back then, we could barely afford to pay ourselves—and often we didn't.

With no venture capital, no fancy pedigrees or insider connections, Lee and I were the quintessential bootstrapping entrepreneurs. It took years of trial and error and diligent effort, but we bootstrapped our way from a tiny, two-person outfit to a respected leader in the digital information space. Together, we had built something extraordinary, and now it felt like the rest of the world was finally recognizing our worth.

But the process of selling a company isn't for the faint of heart. I was exhausted. I'd been wearing the same outfit four days straight because the airline lost my luggage, and I couldn't find a spare moment to go buy a new tee shirt and pants. Lee and I barely had time to eat or sleep. So when the buyer delayed the closing yet again, I decided to fly home the next day and wrap up the deal remotely.

That morning, the deal team assured me the sale would close before I boarded my plane. And then the last of the paperwork *still* wasn't done in time, and I boarded my flight under the gray cloud of another delay. And that's how I found myself 36,000 feet in the air, waiting for the final word on the most improbable and thrilling achievement of my life.

In a happy surprise, the airline had upgraded me to first class. I sat in my plush seat, nervously checking my phone for updates. Still…a big fat nothing. About an hour into the flight, I decided to leave it alone. Maybe it wasn't happening today, just like it hadn't happened five or six other days. With a second glass of champagne in my hand, I reflected on the last two weeks. It seemed endless, this last stretch of the process. Through all our years of struggle and growing the company, I'd never experienced anything so exhausting and stressful. As the champagne took effect, I leaned my head back and closed my eyes, bracing for the worst.

And then the phone pinged. I looked down into the crystal ball of my future—the screen of my cellphone—at an incoming text message: a screenshot of my partner, Lee, with about a dozen other people on a Zoom call. As my eyes focused in on the tiny image, I saw that everyone was smiling…giving the thumbs-up. And then the phone exploded with champagne emoji after champagne emoji after champagne emoji.

The deal was done! Our company had just sold for a staggering $25 million!

The weight of years of constant work and sacrifice seemed to melt from my shoulders. I felt a mixture of joy, relief, exhaustion and disbelief.

Is this really happening? I kept wondering.

I texted my husband and told him to watch our bank account. We were about $200,000 in debt to credit card companies and family members. With his support and encouragement, I'd bet everything on Boardroom Insiders—even though it meant putting our own financial future in limbo. My husband and I needed the money from the sale of the company to make ourselves financially whole again. Giddily, I told him to pay off all our debts as soon as the money hit our bank account.

Within minutes, Andrew texted me a screenshot of our bank balance, which now read over $10 million. Shivers ran through my whole body.

Five minutes after that, he sent me more screenshots: our credit card balances. Some of those cards had had balances of over $30,000. But now every single one had a zero balance.

I could barely contain myself. I was heading home to a clean financial slate and a dramatically changed life.

I thought about how many other people—employees who'd been so loyal to us and had become like family over the years—were now experiencing this same, uncontainable feeling of elation. Lee and I made sure our vested employees would receive equity from the sale. I imagined the ping of bank alerts ricocheting through the office as everyone saw their balances magically skyrocket.

The rest of the flight home felt surreal. It was hard being stuck on a plane with no one to talk to. I wanted to share the moment with someone, anyone. I wanted to grab the woman sitting next to me and yell, "GUESS WHAT? I'M RICH!" But I figured that might be a little crass.

Instead, I asked the flight attendant for another glass of champagne and sat back in my first-class seat, quietly celebrating as I looked out the window at a cloudless blue sky, thinking about how quickly everything can change...

―――――

It was a full year after that plane ride before I realized how astonishingly rare my achievement was.

Of course, I was aware of the gender imbalance in the C-suite, the tech industry and venture funding. Over two decades, I'd had dozens of meetings with venture capitalists, private equity firms, merger-and-acquisitions bankers and corporate development execs—and been the only woman in attendance. It wasn't until I came across some data in 2023 that it really hit me how much the odds are stacked against women in business. And it's not getting much better.

Of the current Fortune 500 companies, women represent only 10.4 percent of CEOs.[1] Women represent only 8.6 percent of all venture capitalists, 8 percent of firm partners (those making the investment decisions and writing checks), and 7 percent of board seats at VC firms—which has a direct impact on the companies funded by venture capital, as fewer than 5 percent have women on their executive teams and only 2.7 percent have a female CEO.[2] When it comes to funding the next wave of American businesses, venture capitalists funneled just 2.1% of their investment dollars to companies with all-female founders in 2023.[3] But...VCs rewarded women *who partnered with men*—the share of venture capital that went to companies with at least one male co-founder increased to 21.7% in 2023, up from 16.5% in 2022.[4] Although women start businesses at more than twice the rate of men, fewer than 2% of female business owners ever make it to $1 million in annual revenue, just one-third the rate of their male peers.[5]

It's no wonder the entrepreneurial stories we hear are almost always told from the perspective of men who create companies worth hundreds of millions and even billions. We rarely hear from women with entrepreneurial dreams who succeed against all odds and create life-changing wealth.

It's time that changed. That's why it's become my mission to make entrepreneurship accessible to everyone, regardless of their background. We now have an opportunity to create our ideal world, where inclusion and access are a birthright—no matter where you're born, or to whom. In this book, you'll be able to trace my steps from a blue-collar world of limiting beliefs that held me in limbo as I struggled to find my way to a successful career, to embracing a new worldview—developing a mindset that helped me break free and believe that success was well within my grasp. As I shrugged off those binds, I not only stood in my power, I empowered everyone around me—by creating a dynamic team to grow the business and cultivating leaders who could stand on their own and create their own success stories.

I know there are more Sharon Gillenwaters out there who can make it to the top, and I'm here to see that they do.

CHAPTER ONE
Blue Collar with a Twist

I GREW up in Ocean Beach, California. This seaside town in San Diego—splendidly depicted in the opening scenes of Cameron Crowe's *Almost Famous*—was beautiful, gritty and wild. In the '60s and '70s, the counterculture scene was big in "OB," as it's commonly known, and my parents forbade me to walk alone on the main street of Newport Avenue—it was full of smoke shops, dive bars, hippies and vagrants. But even in the safe confines of our backyard, I wasn't sheltered from the vibe. I must have been about 10 when the frenetic guitar riff of Led Zeppelin's "Black Dog" came drifting over the fence from the yard next door, like tentacles, one Saturday afternoon. I became transfixed, tiptoeing to the wooden fence and peering through the slats, as I watched my teenage neighbor Tommy and his friends, stoned out of their minds, spinning in circles to the music, eyes closed, their long, tangled hair whirling loose around their bodies.

I felt like I was peering through the looking glass—and it kind of freaked me out. I could tell these kids were out of control, definitely high on something, and that a new era was landing hard in OB, where anything went—and I didn't want any part of it. I never really gravitated to the beach culture either, though I appreciated the beauty of where I lived. There were tons of kids on my block, and I had my friends, but I mostly liked to stay inside and read.

Today, my hometown is cleaner, more gentrified and probably less interesting; its four-block commercial strip is home to a Target, family-friendly restaurants and several microbreweries. While dive bars remain and dispensaries have moved in, their patrons tend to be well-heeled hipsters and tourists. Tommy and his friends have long since moved on, as I did. But OB retained some of its rebellious heritage. In 2022, residents celebrated the closure of a Starbucks on Newport Avenue they never wanted in the first place. "People in OB want to keep OB non-corporate," one resident said.[1]

I'm a first-generation Californian. My dad grew up in Forrest City, Arkansas, which sits between Little Rock and Memphis. His parents had six kids and a working farm, but when he was a teenager, the whole place burned down—and they had no insurance. They lost everything, and the entire family moved west—as far west as they could go. A straight shot from Little Rock would have brought them to LA, but somewhere along the way, they veered south and ended up on Interstate 8, which deposits you right at the gateway to Ocean Beach.

Dad was handsome, outgoing, and charismatic—always fun to be around. He was quick with a joke, and his humor would win you over if his charm didn't. How he went from being a hair stylist in his early days in OB to working at a plating plant for the airlines is a mystery. When he and my mom first met, he was always styling her hair in different ways and applying rinses so she could try out new hair colors.

Mom grew up in Virginia, in extreme poverty. Like my dad, her family lived on a farm, though it was more about subsistence than running a business: her mother slaughtered chickens and hogs, cut firewood and tended the animals and kids, while her dad worked the fields from sun up to sundown. When her mom died of kidney disease when my mother was only 13, she was put in charge of caring for her four brothers and sisters, including an infant. Her father remarried—to a woman who treated her poorly. How poorly? I'll tell it to you the way my mom told it to me: At 18, she paid a visit to the family doctor, and when he saw the condition she was in, he told her to get out of there as fast as she could and never look back. Emaciated and undernourished, she had weighed in at 95 pounds—her bones protruding through her five-foot-seven frame. To this day, my mother does not discuss the details of that time in her life, nor is she in contact with anyone in her family.

Mom took the doctor's advice and set out on her own. First, she went to Florida to stay with a friend who was a flight attendant. She considered working for the airlines, but an infestation of beastly palmetto bugs in her girlfriend's apartment sent her packing. Traveling by bus to San Diego (which has very few bugs), she moved into the YWCA downtown. There, she met my dad's sister, Mary, who worked at the naval base in Coronado, in human resources, and hired my mom to work in the computer programming department. Computer work was largely clerical back then, and therefore considered suitable "women's work." Mom handled the era's memorable "punch cards," which were fed into computers for data intake: each hole punched into a card represented letters or numbers.

Before too long, Mom's male bosses noticed her work ethic and natural talent and sent her to Los Angeles to train with IBM, the pioneer of both business and personal computing. Mom was overjoyed. She lacked a college education and had had so few opportunities in life so far. This seemed like a really big break—and indeed, it was. She ended up working as a civilian computer programmer for the Navy for the next 30 years, steadily promoted until she was working alongside younger peers with master's degrees.

I admired my mom's professional wardrobe. She wore smart dresses and heels, pantyhose, trendy costume jewelry and sometimes even wigs. I liked the idea that people dressed for the office, and I looked forward to that kind of future for myself. Mom also gave me my first exposure to computers and technology. Sometimes called into the office in the middle of the night or on weekends to "fix a hang," as she called it, she'd take me with her. I'd play with the discarded punch cards, and she'd make a bed for me on top of a gray, metal, government-issued desk—with blankets and pillows brought from home. My dad worked nights, so she had no choice, but they were special moments I'll never forget.

My admiration wasn't limited to mom's sartorial style. It always impressed me that she worked on sophisticated technology alongside colleagues with advanced degrees even though she had no college education herself. She was one of our nation's early cybersecurity professionals, detecting and deflecting bugs and worms that could do our nation harm. She didn't mind working at night or on weekends, or whenever she was needed. She loved her job and her colleagues and enjoyed her work. I imagined a future like that for myself; I figured if she did it, I could too.

She bonded with the few other women in her workplace, and they'd go to lunch and visit each other on weekends. But their bosses were universally men. Once, when my mom applied for a promotion, she was told flat out that the position was a "man's job" and she wouldn't be considered. Blatant misogyny was fairly standard in her time, but she harbored no bitterness. I think it was hard for her to recognize: it was just the way things were, and she never let it get under her skin.

Mom sometimes attended tech conferences in San Francisco, such as Oracle's OpenWorld Conference, where I once tagged along as her plus-one when I was in college. Standing on the expansive lawn of Oracle's headquarters overlooking San Francisco Bay, I was in awe of the scale of the Bay Area and the opulence of the party, impressed by my mother's place in this world, never imagining that decades later, I'd be attending the same events.

Mom retired early, but not because of sexism; it was the corruption she couldn't abide. Serving on an oversight panel that selected technology vendors for lucrative government contracts, she blew the whistle when a panel member's cronyism steered a big contract to the least qualified vendor. When her concerns were brushed aside and the vendor retaliated against her, she resigned in protest. She had wanted to work longer to rack up her pension, but she was 52 and it was a tough time: my dad was fighting cancer, so she didn't need the extra stress or aggravation. When she quit in 1991, she was making around sixty grand a year. Given how hard her youth had been and the fact that she had never gone to college, it was an amazing achievement.

As an only child, I'm pretty sure I was unplanned. My mom wanted to make sure I got the best of everything, and I think she worried that working hampered her ability to manage my upbringing. So she put me in a private elementary school, despite the cost. My grandparents took care of me before and after school. Mom would take me to their apartment before she went to work, and I'd have breakfast with them—always instant oatmeal. Then Grandpa would take me out to the sidewalk, and we'd wait for the school bus.

It was a great little school a few blocks from the beach, and I loved it. Classes were small, and we were taught Spanish every day. The Spanish teacher, Mrs. Diaz, was an elegant older woman from Mexico. She wore bright pink lipstick, poncho-style sweaters and had a dramatic gray streak through her beautifully coiffed dark hair. Mrs. Diaz lived right next door to the school and worked out of a little cottage on our tiny campus, which everyone called "The Spanish Cottage." She filled her classroom with colorful objects (for teaching the names of colors), full place settings (for meal-related vocabulary) and papier-mâché fruits and vegetables as visual aids. It was foundational for me.

Given that I was in a private school, most of my schoolmates came from wealthy families—or families far more well-off than mine, anyway. One lived in a huge house that spanned two blocks, so they had two completely different addresses—the back door was on one street and the front door on another. I'd never seen anything like it! Every year, that family would host events like mother-daughter teas and a massive Easter egg hunt. My school friends' parents were executives, doctors, lawyers and successful entrepreneurs.

The disparities in our lifestyles made me realize that even though my family was perfectly comfortable and wanted for nothing, we were from the proverbial "other side of the tracks." And seeing how wealthy people lived turned me into a striver with a dream to cross those tracks.

I loved reading, studying, singing and acting. And I'd sometimes get involved in things my parents found odd—things that were outside their worldview—like joining a rock band and traveling solo to out-of-the-way places. My father just didn't take an interest, but my mom was often the voice of dissent, or at least of caution. It's not that she wasn't supportive; but there was a finite box into which life fit for her, and she couldn't see outside it. She couldn't imagine a bigger life and didn't understand why I would forsake something safe for something risky. My parents' inability to see beyond that box impeded my sense of adventure. I broke out of the box in my own way but was still tethered to it by their beliefs. I was taught never to dream too big, so I wouldn't be disappointed.

Though my mother was the primary breadwinner of our family, that didn't mean my father was progressive. He was a blue-collar guy, and though mom worked a full-time job, he still expected her to do all the cooking, cleaning, shopping and anything having to do with child-rearing. He took the money she earned and bought run-down apartment buildings, fixing them up to rent. He was happiest puttering around in the garage and cruising around Ocean Beach in his van, checking on his buildings and tenants.

My father had a strong personality, with a knack for calling out stupidity when he saw it. His tenants tended to be a little afraid of him. I should know; I was one of them. I lived in one of his buildings for a time, and while he charged me rent, he did give me a discount. Once I heard him haranguing my neighbor, who was on his third replacement garbage disposal: "You do *know*," my dad griped, "that you can't put *rocks* in there!" Dad had no filter.

He fit right in in his adopted town. Looking like any of the other middle-aged hippies on Newport Avenue, he wore only shorts, had longish hair and kept a beard and sideburns. His belief system, however, was more conservative; he could be bigoted and sexist. He'd worked in the plating shop for an airline, dipping massive engine parts into swimming-pool-sized vats of chemicals and sometimes working the night shift. My mom says that a lot of guys who worked in that plant ended up dying of cancer—she believes it's what killed him. Dad quit his job long before he got sick and started buying properties to rent out—not out of concern for his health but because he could not stand working for anyone else. More than anything, this stemmed from his temperament. He was emotionally volatile, to the point that I wasn't comfortable bringing friends over to the house. It wasn't easy being an only child, walking on eggshells. I never knew when his temper was going to flare. I loved my parents and was proud of them both, but given Dad's unpredictability, I ended up spending most of my childhood in my room reading, or over at friends' houses.

I was lucky to have several other strong female role models in my family. My dad's four sisters were all real badasses. I wonder today if their resourcefulness and resilience was rooted in the loss of the family farm, which led to all of them fleeing Arkansas and starting over. The eldest, Christine, founded and ran her own real estate company in San Antonio. Mary worked her way up from hospital volunteer to hospital executive in Los Angeles. Peggy became a special education teacher and advocate in San Diego. And Betty put herself through college, then worked her way up to chief financial officer of a publicly traded company—all while raising their kids.

Betty and Mary lived not too far from one another in LA. In my early 20s, I loved to drive up and visit them for a few days. They always made time for me, taking me out to nice restaurants in Pasadena and insisting on paying for everything. I loved getting to know my aunts as people, and we always had a great time. Despite having to leave for the office at dawn, Betty was always up for discussing work and politics late into the night over a good bottle of wine. And though she was a single mom, her week revolved primarily around work.

Aunt Betty was tough, had a wicked sense of humor and could dish for hours about workplace "bullshit." I loved her stories, which always made me laugh. One afternoon, I drove up to LA and used a hidden key to let myself into her house. I kicked off my shoes, opened a bottle of Chardonnay and waited for her to come home. After changing into a stylish sweatsuit, she settled into her fluffy, white down sofa, legs curled under her, white wine in hand.

"You know," she said, "I was in my office this morning, and this guy came in to complain about *something*, going on and on and on…*blah, blah, blah*…and all I could think about was how I'd had not *one* but *two* unusually large bowel movements before I left the house…" Aunt Betty was one of a kind.

I was lucky to have a working mother and powerhouse aunts as role models. They were a rare breed in those days. My circle of elementary school friends had only one other working mom, who also happened to work in computing at the naval base.

As the years wore on, Dad could get borderline abusive toward my mom sometimes, and it didn't sit well with me. Even as a little kid, I'd call him out, yelling at him when he got out of line. He came and went as he pleased. He stayed out late if he felt like it—doing who knows what. Maybe he was at the bar with friends, or even with another woman. He'd cheated on my mom once before.

One such night, he came home drunk, in a foul mood about something. Mom and I were already asleep, and we woke up to his ranting and swearing.

Bang!

"Son of a bitch! Stupid piece of shit!"

Neither of us paid him any mind. Been here, done this.

As I turned over and tried to go back to sleep, I heard him turning on every faucet in the house, full blast.

You've got to be effing kidding me.

Then the television switched on, and the radio...all full volume, until the entire house was pulsating.

That's it!

I flew out of bed, banging my knee on the dresser. "God damnit!"

First to the bathroom, then the kitchen—I turned everything off—and found him in the living room, still pacing.

"Dad! You've got to be kidding me! What is *wrong* with you?"

He was a mess, drunk and pissed off, looking like a cat that had been left out in the rain—his stained bomber jacket askew on his shoulders, hair a rat's-nest mess.

"Dad! I'm talking to you!"

"What, Sharon—for chrissakes!? Leave me..." He trailed off, looking at me like he'd never realized I was growing up.

"Why are you doing this? Look at you! This is so stupid! Shame on you!"

And in a flash, his rage turned to tears. He fell back onto the sofa, one hand over his face, the other fighting with his coat.

"I'm sorry, hon, I…" The weeping took his breath. "Oh, shit…"

I crept off to bed as he broke down crying.

I never fully understood his anger. Even now, as an adult, I have a hard time fathoming where his rage came from… though I *can* tell you I inherited his temper. It takes a lot to tick me off, but when somebody does: I've heard it ain't pretty.

After the night of noise, we had more and more confrontations, and they made him cry every time.

One day, I came home from school and found mom warding off another verbal assault, busying herself in the kitchen as he lambasted her with criticism about something or another.

"What's going on?"

"Nothing, honey," my mom gave me "the look."

"No, uh-uh." I shook my head.

I'd seen Dad shuffling off to the living room when I came in, but I was done. I tracked him down, hands on hips.

"Dad, what's the problem?" I pinned him with my eyes.

His lips moved, but nothing came out of his mouth.

"Why are you yelling at mom? Again?!"

I wasn't going to let him get away with berating my mother anymore.

"Do you have something to say?"

Again, his lips moved, but all that came out this time was a sob.

I have a thing about justice—if something is wrong, it must be rectified.

The next time he threw a tantrum, I shut it down and cornered my mom.

"Why do you let him get away with this? It's ridiculous. Why don't you just tell him off?"

"Sharon, honey, it's just not worth the aggravation. I let him rant, he gets it out of his system, and life goes on."

It frustrated me that I had to be the one to put a stop to the madness while she did nothing to stand up to him.

"Well, that's insane. I can't stand this anymore!"

Mom would make excuses. Dad had gotten rheumatic fever as a child, which damaged his heart. The doctors predicted he would not survive very far into adulthood—so his four sisters doted on him, spoiling him, she explained.

"Who cares? Why not break the dysfunctional pattern then? You don't deserve to be treated this way!"

My dad did mellow over time, though I am not sure why. He eventually bought a piece of property in the heart of Ocean Beach that housed a lone cottage, and he used the rest of the lot to build a proper home for my mom and him so they'd have a little view of the beach. And that was where they lived until he died.

I inherited traits from each of my parents: I have my father's big feelings and my mom's work ethic. But there was a part of me that was always searching for something more...something different.

My little school by the sea went through sixth grade. So from seventh through 12th grades, I attended The Bishop's School, a private school 30 minutes up the coast—and a world away, really—in La Jolla, California. Knowing what I know now, I can't believe my mom pulled it off financially. Bishop's was the kind of school attended by the superrich—kids of celebrities, socialites, business tycoons and wealthy families from Asia and Latin America. I begged my mom to let me go to Bishop's because all of my elementary school friends were going. She didn't bother consulting with my dad—she knew he'd be against it: Why did I have to run with this wealthy crowd? They were wonderful people, and he didn't even know them, but that's what he would have said. Maybe he was intimidated by their success and money.

Dad had never been involved in my school life or the decision-making about my education, which was not unusual for dads of that era. He left it all to my mom, which meant she could do what she wanted and make my dream of staying with my friends come true. Tuition was four grand a year in 1977. I could have gotten financial aid—my grades were good enough to get me a scholarship, and my parents didn't make a lot of money—but it didn't even occur to my mom to apply for it. She was making a good living—why would she ask for help? My family maintained a conservative attitude that such things were handouts, and we didn't take handouts. While she might have thought it ridiculous that I'd go to such an expensive school, she always bent over backward for me. She ended up taking out loans she never told my father about.

On top of paying my tuition, my mother had to find a way to get me there every day. It could take over a half an hour by car and then she would have to double back and drive nearly an hour to work, and there was no bus service. So we had to rely on the kindness of strangers.

The majority of my co-eds were from wealthy families—so wealthy that it was impossible not to see the chasm between our lifestyles. Even so, *no one* was riding to school in a Rolls-Royce...except for my friend Wendy. Wendy's mom owned the Rolls. When she drove it, she'd talk about how much she hated the car, inherited from her wealthy father-in-law. She called it The Pig. But they didn't get rid of it.

The Pig was midnight blue, and riding in it was like floating on a cloud. How do I know? Wendy's mom offered to drive me to school every day! Sitting in the back seat, I stared out the window at the world going by, using the little fold-down tray (just like I was on an airplane). It was made of gorgeous, burled wood—I can still see it in my mind's eye. Everything was made of wood or rich leather, beautifully crafted and polished. The seats were deep and cushy, and the car smelled like the luxury only money can buy.

Not only were people staring at us when we pulled up at school, they were staring at us throughout the entire drive. It was absurd...and a little embarrassing. Imagine you're in seventh grade and you're starting at a brand-new school. You already feel awkward—your hair's greasy, your skin's a mess, you feel ugly—and all you want to do is blend in, or disappear altogether. The last thing you want is to attract attention. Well, there's no escaping attention when you pull up to school in a Rolls every day. I didn't want people knowing I was from "the wrong side of the tracks." Spending so much time alone as a kid because of my father's volatility, I was already socially awkward, and I didn't want to be pegged as a scholarship kid. But I didn't want to be known as the rich girl either.

Or did I?

CHAPTER TWO
Jobs and Internships

"WHAT ARE YOUR QUALIFICATIONS, Sharon? What makes you a good fit for this position?"

Was this guy leering at me, or...?

"Um, well, I'm a hard worker. And a quick study. And I don't mind getting my hands dirty."

Oh my God, what an idiotic thing to say...Now he's definitely leering.

"How do you feel about after-hours work?"

"Yeah! I'm willing to do whatever it takes to get the job done."

Shit! Did I really just say that? Get me out of here.

"Hmm." Serge tented his fingers and smiled knowingly, his jacket squeaking as he leaned back into his chair. "And how do you feel about being chased around the desk just a little?"

Holy shit...

"Just kidding, Sharon—hey! You've got the job! Congratulations!"

It was a doozy, but that was my first interview for a real job —and the actual job that followed wasn't much better.

I started college in 1982, having set my sights on UC San

Diego, majoring in communications and sociology. With graduation about a year away, I was determined to get some work experience that would put me on the path to a good job. Up to that point, the only jobs I'd had were scooping ice cream and waiting tables. During college, I rented a house with four friends in a sleepy little beach community called Leucadia. I waited tables at the local pie shop, and three of my housemates worked at the same place. We made enough in pay and tips to get by, so life was fairly easy. But at the age of 20, with a college degree imminent, I was looking forward to starting a real career.

The problem was, I had no clue what I wanted to do—I didn't know what jobs were out there or how to get them. My strategy had always been to take any job I could get to support myself. I believed that the harder I worked, the more money I'd make. In high school, I worked at Baskin-Robbins; in college, I worked at a gift shop, a pie shop and then a seafood restaurant. Those jobs made sense at the time—they put cash in my pocket and had flexible hours, allowing me to pick up more shifts if I needed more money.

I enjoyed the camaraderie I had with the waitstaff, bartenders, busboys and cooks, and they taught me the importance of teamwork. Since I often befriended my coworkers, my personal and professional lives intersected smoothly, which was a godsend. I had to make friends at work—I didn't have time to meet people any other way! Being shy in social situations, it took me a long time to open up. But once I did, I forged strong connections.

The restaurant industry was hard work, something I excelled at and enjoyed. I liked the feeling of time evaporating when I was so busy I could barely keep pace. That desire to stay busy never left me, and I hated any job where I had to stand around waiting for orders or feedback. Boredom would set in, my mind would wander and I'd find myself with disturbing thoughts, worrying about my future amidst all the darkness in the world.

Other than pay, my criteria for taking on jobs were whether they seemed enjoyable or had requirements I could easily meet. I didn't make strategic choices, network or do anything proactive—and sometimes, it bit me in the ass.

Prior to my interview with Serge in 1986, I'd applied for two internships—one at an advertising and PR firm looking for someone to write copy about Jazzercise, the fitness craze that was sweeping the country at the time, and the other at *San Diego Magazine*, a glossy, monthly periodical covering issues and happenings around the city. I heard from the ad firm first and got the gig. It would be my first experience of sexual harassment in a professional setting.

Located in a generic business park on the outskirts of the city, the firm had about 15 employees, and the vibe was uninspiring and dreary. I was given a small desk in a windowless corner, where I spent hours writing peppy headlines and copy for Jazzercise ads. Even though I was a fitness buff and had done Jazzercise many times, I found the work mind-numbing. I was, however, grateful to be doing something other than waiting tables.

The owner, Serge, was a short, mustachioed man who wore a black leather aviator jacket like it was his business suit. Serge thankfully never chased me around the office (and never expanded on what he might've done if he'd caught me), but his jokes just kept coming. Since he never acted on them, it fell under the category of "inappropriate behavior" rather than crossing the line into out-and-out sexual harassment. But it didn't matter. I'd become used to unwanted attention from restaurant customers and managers. I'd also been in a rock band and knew how men talked about women when they thought we weren't listening. My girlfriends all had similar experiences at work, and we often shared our tales of harassment with each other. Swapping stories and laughing at the perps helped us cope.

I shared my first apartment with a friend from UCSD named Sheila. Occasionally, our panties were stolen from the dryers in the complex's laundry room. One day, we found a large manila envelope on our doorstep containing several black-and-white 8x10 photos of an erect penis from various angles. Looking back, we probably should have called the police. That's what I would want my own daughter to do. Instead, we cracked up, tears running down our faces until we were breathless. Then Sheila stuck them in a drawer, and we forgot about them. I still see Sheila once in a while, and the incident is as hilarious to us now as it was forty years ago. Unfortunately, for young women starting their adult lives in the 1980s, this was pretty routine stuff.

My first business lunch took place at a steakhouse that was more like a glorified strip club. When Serge invited me there, I was naïve enough to think he was interested in offering me a full-time, paid position. At noon, we walked across the parking lot in the hot sun, the pavement seeming to melt as my nerves kicked up with anticipation. He ushered me into a steakhouse sandwiched between a nail shop and a car stereo store in an unremarkable concrete strip mall. The interior was like a vault —so dimly lit that it was impossible to tell if it was day or night outside and adorned with heavy brown curtains and neon beer signs. We settled into a circular red Naugahyde booth. A group of men sat at the bar, drinking cocktails.

The seediness of the place gave me the creeps, but I was nonetheless nervous and excited, hoping that the meeting would result in more hours or responsibility—and maybe even some pay. Serge sat back, draping his aviator-jacket-clad arms across the booth. He grinned at me and nodded his head, comfy in his lair. We made small talk, then ordered lunch. Suddenly, the music in the restaurant got louder—a smooth and sexy jazz, heavy on the sax—and a woman appeared on a stage that jutted out into the middle of an aisle between the booths. She was dressed in red lingerie. Two more women followed her, dressed in similar getups. The show went on for about 15 minutes, the women slithering on and off the runway stage, changing into different lingerie sets each time they emerged.

I looked around—the other booths were filled with businessmen eating meat, sipping martinis and devouring the eye candy. Had my boss intentionally brought me to a lingerie show at a strip club? I was 20 years old, and I didn't know if this was normal, so I pretended it was—acting like I was cool with it, casually chewing on my burger, slowly realizing that this outing wasn't going to result in any career development.

Once I accepted this, I tuned Serge out, and my mind wandered to the business model behind the unfolding spectacle. My curiosity went into overdrive and I had a million questions. How much were these girls getting paid? How did they get the gig? Did they like it? How was the restaurant recouping their wages? Were they selling enough food and drink to cover the cost? Did anyone actually buy lingerie at these things—and if so, did the restaurant get a cut? Maybe the restaurateur's brother had a lingerie company and that's how this freak show happened? If one of the male diners did buy some lingerie, how would he explain the purchase to his wife or girlfriend? "Well honey, I was having lunch with the guys from the office, and they just *happened* to have a little lingerie show..." Ick. Somebody please explain to me how this could possibly end well!

I put in a total of three months at the agency before leaving for another internship at *San Diego Magazine*. I never saw Serge again, though I have to say, I've never forgotten him.

San Diego Magazine was a breath of fresh air: there was a long list of editorial projects, the editors piled on as much responsibility as I was capable of handling and the whole place was run by women. In those early days of my internship, I wasn't doing any writing, but the expectations were clear, and my purposeful. I spent my days on the phone, fact-c calling to verify dates and times of social events around the ci̇, It was a never-ending loop: when I was done calling and logging one month's events, it was time to start again for next month's issue.

After a couple of months, I became concerned I could get trapped doing this work indefinitely. But two women in the editorial department took notice of me, offering new opportunities and responsibilities. They could not have been more different, but both would become my mentors, and in their unique ways, influence the integrity of my work and help me navigate a professional setting.

Soon, I was given my first writing assignment. Thrilled at the chance to write a breezy little 300-word article about upcoming events in a section called "Urban Eye," I quickly realized that as a feature writer, I was pretty green. I could write clearly and coherently enough, but I didn't know how to write compellingly, concisely and with nuance. This is where Virginia "Ginny" Butterfield changed my life.

Ginny, one of the senior editors at the magazine, took me under her wing, taking time to review and edit my work and explaining her changes with me at her side. She was a masterful editor, using a red pencil and all of the copyediting symbols of the trade, a shorthand I soaked up. Her edits clicked for me—I saw how they instantly made my pieces better. And because I came to understand what Ginny wanted, I got better and faster in no time, able to deliver and meet deadlines.

Ginny was tough, but she was also witty, kindhearted and fair. She was direct, and sometimes her blunt assessments of my work hurt my feelings, but she had high standards and expected the same of others. She was also beautiful, glamorous and urbane—so much so that she seemed out of place in our gritty beach burg. I wasn't surprised to learn that early in her career, she'd lived and worked in New York City. Writing for television in the nascent days of the medium, she left the field after marrying a network executive and having five children. Her husband died suddenly on the golf course one day, leaving her a single mom with no steady income.

So Ginny went back to work, writing and editing for magazines. Still a city person at heart, she lived in a small condo in downtown San Diego, decades before it became fashionable. She'd take the junior staff out for lunch and tell them stories of her life and career. Her kids were adults now, and while no one in the office knew how old she was, it was a topic of much speculation. Her life experience made me think she must be about 75, but she looked like she was in her mid-50s. She never said it herself, but she was a survivor—a woman who cared for her children and built a new career at an age when most people were thinking about retirement.

Ginny believed in doing your research and locking down all the little details so you could defend your work. I learned that lesson the hard way. Shortly after I'd been hired full-time as a junior editor, Ginny asked me to go shopping to select a book to give as a farewell gift to our departing interns. I drove to a nearby bookstore, briefly browsed the covers of a few writing books, selected one and grabbed a few copies. My task completed, I left the books on Ginny's desk.

Later that afternoon, Ginny stepped into my office. I could tell something was wrong because she was wearing her reading glasses low on her nose, looking over them at me with one of the books in her hand. In her elegant voice, she asked, "Sharon, did you happen to peruse this book at all?" I admitted that I'd only read the dust jacket. She opened the book and pointed out the title of Chapter Three: "Why Your Editor Is an Idiot." I felt my face grow hot.

I respected and adored Ginny, so I was horrified at having disappointed her. Learning the importance of rigorous due diligence was a game-changing life lesson. From then on, I was fully prepared to defend any decision I made—double-checking everything and verifying my work.

I also watched Ginny pick her battles and sometimes win them in her inimitable way. Once, one of the owners of the magazine became fascinated by a company that allowed people to name a star after a loved one as a gift—for a hefty fee. Ginny thought it was a nonsensical scam and was loath to give it one word of ink. For a couple of weeks, she managed to ignore the owner's request that she personally write a blurb about it. But the owner didn't back off, and Ginny was forced to comply. I sat in her office as she angrily banged away at her keyboard, narrating her copy out loud. She blazed through the vexing assignment, writing the whole thing in about five minutes.

Her copy was breezy and polished, but I detected a slight whiff of finespun ridicule that only those who knew Ginny would recognize. Today, I can recall only one line, which I can still hear in her velvety, patrician voice: "*Some* people say they make great *gifts!*"

I'd never had someone with Ginny's talent and rich life experience take an interest in me, and the fact that she thought I was worthy of her mentorship boosted my confidence. It was a gift I vowed to pass on if I ever found myself in the situation of leading young people.

Ginny was not my only mentor at the magazine, which had an abundance of female leadership. Another editor, Maribeth Mellin, supervised all the interns, so I had a lot of contact with her. As smart and nurturing as Ginny, she could not have been more different. Maribeth lived in Ocean Beach in a tidy Spanish-style bungalow, where she cultivated a magnificent flower garden. While most of the neighborhood cottages were fronted by small patches of lawn, her yard was a wild and vibrant tangle of blooms—sunflowers, poppies and roses of every color. My favorite were the dahlias. I had never seen one before I set foot in her garden, and I was enchanted by them. Every summer now, I visit the spectacular dahlia garden in San Francisco's Golden Gate Park, and I always think of Maribeth.

Maribeth was hip and progressive. She wore colorful, flowing caftans and dusters and practiced yoga decades before it was ubiquitous in urban centers and suburban strip malls. Hailing from Washington, DC, she cared deeply about politics and social justice and became an investigative journalist of consequence in San Diego. I should have been intimidated by her, but she was affable, approachable and genuinely enjoyed spending time with the younger staff, whom she treated as peers. We lunched at the Chinese restaurant next door to the office, the Greek taverna down the street or the fish taco joint nearby. We also enjoyed happy hours by the beach. To my cohort of 20-something "peons" working our first real jobs at the magazine, Maribeth was a trusted ally, someone we all wanted to spend time with despite the fact that she was more than a decade older.

Maribeth drove a vintage, cherry-red Volvo sedan—not the mom kind, but a jazzy little two-door coupe. No one else in the city had a car like hers, so it was easy for me to spot her all over town. One day, she forgot to set the emergency brake, and the car rolled down the street away from her bungalow—making a wide arc and eventually coming to rest against a neighbor's pickup truck. When the owner of the truck—a tall, handsome, bearded fisherman named Gary—knocked on her door to ask her to come claim her car, they were both smitten. My *San Diego Magazine* colleagues and I attended their wedding—an outdoor affair that concluded with the newlyweds walking through a saber arch—but instead of swords, Gary's friends held fishing poles aloft. He and Maribeth still live in that Spanish bungalow in Ocean Beach.

Ginny and Maribeth took their work seriously but approached the inevitable office politics and absurdities with lightness and amusement. They knew we weren't curing cancer, and that nothing about a city magazine was worth getting bent out of shape over. We had fun, and I loved every minute of it. The pay was paltry—even for a 26-year-old in 1991—but the job had its perks: free events almost every night, like restaurant openings, cocktail parties and hotel stays. It was the perfect way for a young adult on a shoestring budget to see more of what the world had to offer. But after four years, my salary was only $15,000, and I was barely scraping by. I could make more money waiting tables than writing restaurant reviews or articles like "Ninety-One San Diegans to Watch in 1991." It was time to move on, though I didn't know where to go—and was about to go through another pivotal event that would take my life in a new direction.

Dad had been undergoing cancer treatment for two years, but despite his aggressive course of chemo, his cancer kept spreading, and he was getting progressively worse. We knew he wasn't going to make it about three months before he died, and he spent the last month at home in hospice, in the house he had built for my mom and him. I'd prepared myself for his death, but one can never fully be ready for such a loss. I was still pretty young, trying to figure out who I was and what I wanted. About six months before he passed away, I told him I was thinking of quitting *San Diego Magazine*. When he asked me why, I said I just wasn't enjoying the work anymore.

"Sharon!" he replied. "It's *work*! You're not supposed to *like* it!"

I put off quitting until after he was gone so he wouldn't be disappointed in me. While my dad could be volatile and unpredictable—and we didn't have a ton in common—there was never any doubt that he adored me. He loved me through and through. That's why he used to cry when I would scream at him for misbehaving. And though I experienced his death as a relief because of the way he suffered, I had no regrets.

The last few months were hard. My mom and I spent a lot of time with him in the hospital, then at home in hospice care. When he died before dawn one January morning, that sense of relief came rushing through, like a welcome stranger. I even went to work that day. Work has always been useful for me—either to focus, or to distract. It defines me and gives me purpose. That day, it gave me solace. The day of the biggest loss of my life, I headed into the office, knowing full well I would soon be saying goodbye to it—and all the wonderful mentors and friends I'd made over the course of those four years.

I realized I could work from anywhere, and I was itching to escape San Diego for a while. I'd been to Europe after college and loved it, so I decided to return and try my hand at travel writing. Leaving Mom behind so soon after Dad's death wasn't an easy decision, but she encouraged me to go. And given that I felt at a professional standstill, I wanted to shake things up.

I picked up some writing work before I left. The freelance community in San Diego embraced me as one of its newest members. I noticed the freelancers who succeeded financially were the ones always hustling for gigs. The most talented and well connected received regular assignments from big, prestigious publications like the *LA Times* or *New York Times*. Others were willing to mix in corporate and PR writing and editing assignments, which paid better than editorial. I suspected I had neither the talent nor the experience to get the more prestigious assignments, and I wasn't sure I was willing to work hard enough to get there. So I cobbled together a patchwork of projects from news services, corporate copywriting, PR and the like. I figured that with enough clients, I could make a decent living while working on my own time and schedule. The challenge was getting my foot in the door.

Maribeth always had a side hustle to supplement her magazine salary, and she helped me get my first freelance gigs. She was writing for Fodor's travel guides and hired me to do the grunt work of calling hotels and restaurants to update their information. That gig led to my writing copy for Fodor's, which led to an assignment to write an entire book on Southern California theme parks. With the exception of Sea World (which I considered cruelty to animals), I loved theme parks, so it was a dream come true: I was going to Disneyland, Knott's Berry Farm and Magic Mountain for free *and* getting paid to do it, with a budget to try all the parks' different restaurants!

Then I spent six months traveling through Europe in the second half of 1991. Using London as a base, I traveled to France, Czechoslovakia, Switzerland, through the UK and Ireland. I managed to sell about a half dozen articles, including one on London's hidden bookstores that was featured in the *San Francisco Chronicle*. It wasn't much—a couple hundred bucks here and there—but it felt good to have it coming in as I made my way around the continent. And while it was gratifying, I couldn't afford to continue traveling with what I was getting paid to write. Finding a full-time job abroad was nearly impossible because of visa requirements, so I returned to the US.

At that point, everything had come full circle. I'd worked in real jobs and sharpened my skills as a researcher and writer. I learned to find and manage clients and deliver what they needed. But I was 27 years old and barely making enough money to support myself. So I did what a lot of people do at that point—I looked at graduate school.

CHAPTER THREE
The Transition to Tech

BETWEEN FREELANCING, studying for the GRE, looking at potential graduate schools and even going on the occasional date, my life was full. And I began to notice a recurring theme: I didn't have a path or a plan. During my stint as a freelancer, I took on all kinds of assignments—PR, corporate writing, travel guides and feature articles. Every project, every client was different. And I applied the same scattershot approach to looking at grad schools. I didn't really know what I wanted to do, so how could I possibly know what I wanted to study?

Then I came across the International Relations and Pacific Studies program at UC San Diego, where I'd earned my undergraduate degree. I loved the campus, and I was intrigued by doing something in international business, so I applied and was accepted. When it came to setting long-term goals, I was still treading water, but at least I had a plan for the next two years. I could keep freelancing to earn money while earning my degree.

The program was only about three years old, and it had two tracks: public sector and policymaking, and international business and investment banking. The curriculum covered economics, statistics, policy analysis and international business. I was more interested in the business classes, and I loved the

fact that I needed to pass a language proficiency test to graduate. This allowed me to continue my lifelong pursuit of Spanish
fluency.

The program was grueling, and I was most definitely among
the black sheep. Several of us were creatively inclined and not
interested in working at the World Bank or in the investment
banking sector. We worked in small groups, and my group
endeavored to make presentations more lively and irreverent.
Our approach was generally well-received, but a couple of our
professors disapproved—mistaking our ingenuity for insin-
cerity—and believed we weren't taking the work seriously

Classes were taught in the Socratic method, and students
would be called on randomly to answer questions or otherwise
demonstrate their knowledge. This kept everyone engaged...
and terrified. Best case: you get called on to talk about a topic
you know really well—a welcome opportunity for intellectual
peacocking. Worst case: you get caught flat-footed and fall on
your face. I tried to memorize everything to make sure I'd be
prepared. But after a while, I realized that while familiarity with
the material was important, the more critical skill was knowing
how to think on my feet—and I began to enjoy the challenge. I
also learned that when I didn't know the answer or the topic, it
was better to admit it than make an ass of myself and waste
everyone's time. Publicly admitting one's ignorance is something to be respected, not scorned.

A pillar of the program was a two-semester international
business simulation course, which we called ISL. Groups were
formed, and each assumed the identity of a country or a
company, with one group representing the media. Countries
were charged with making policy decisions, companies with
business decisions, and the media reported and analyzed it all. I
joined the media team, along with five other grad school "mis-
fits." We had a blast unleashing our creative skills, publishing a
printed weekly newsletter and recording news broadcasts. Our

professors didn't love what we were doing and wouldn't grant the modest production funding we needed. Undeterred, we held weekly bake sales to raise money to meet our budget. I formed lifelong friendships with everyone on the team. But we soon found ourselves in the center of a scandal.

In addition to our role as the media, ISL case study assignments were mandatory for every student and group, and they involved crunching a lot of numbers in Excel. I had never used Excel before, and no one in our group was great at quantitative analysis, so we were always tearing our hair out over these assignments. We were supposed to work on the case studies in our groups, but we weren't allowed to share our spreadsheet work—each of us had to have our own discrete spreadsheet.

After we turned in our case studies, certain members of my group, including me, were accused of cheating—an accusation that could prevent us from graduating. My tenacity for righting wrongs kicked in. The professors' accusation was unfair and unfounded, and when someone goes after me like that, God help them. If we didn't disprove the accusation, one of my teammates—who had already repeated one year of the program—would have to repeat another year or drop out. We were innocent, and I set out to prove it.

We'd worked on the assignment in the campus computer lab, where we'd print out our spreadsheets, edit them, make revisions on the computer, then throw the printouts into a recycling bin the size of an oil barrel. I charged into the computer lab, emptied the bin into a giant garbage bag and brought everything home to my apartment. Digging through every piece of paper, I found each of our draft spreadsheets, compared them to our digital files and taped together the relevant printouts. Then we asked for a meeting with the professors. Using the spreadsheets as visual aids, we proved that the work was unique to each individual. The professors had to write a letter of apology, and we were all vindicated and graduated the following June.

I am harder on myself than anyone, and my integrity is rock solid. I also suffer from chronic self-doubt and insecurity, which has held me back in certain ways—so I don't need anyone else bringing me down, especially with false accusations. The incident was traumatic for me, and I spent hours analyzing those spreadsheets to prove our innocence and secure our rightful place at graduation. All because a couple of professors didn't like our style. But they underestimated our tenacity and the fierceness with which we would defend ourselves. I rarely think of the incident now, and I'm not a vindictive person, but if my alma mater ever calls for a donation, I'll say, "I'll pass. And let me tell you why..." I wonder if those professors ever took a moment of self-reflection after we proved our innocence.

In grad school, I also learned how to collaborate in small groups and craft effective presentations, two skills that would serve me well as I embarked on a new business career in a new city. I never thought I could become a good presenter, but with the help of my professors and fellow students, my confidence grew, and I even began to enjoy it. My formula for success has remained the same to this day, and it consists of two things: mastery of the material, and preparation—which means predicting and fleshing out potential questions and objections. Whether I'm presenting to a client, an investor or a board, I'm always anticipating what might derail me. Preparation gives me confidence, extinguishes fear and makes me excited to share what I know with my audience. But I'm pragmatic too: if I'm walking into a low-risk scenario because I know the topic well, I don't expend as much time preparing because I'm unlikely to be tripped up.

One thing I wasn't quite prepared for was meeting Andrew. Even after I left *San Diego Magazine*, I continued to run in the same editorial circles and still got invited to all the big restaurant openings and parties. I'd seen Andrew around—you really couldn't miss him: tall and quiet with an enigmatic grin, he always wore a fedora. One evening, my friend Susan and I were on our way to the opening of a huge restaurant on the waterfront.

"I wonder if that Andrew will show up," Susan jogged her eyebrows and grinned.

"Yeah...who *is* that guy?" I said. "I keep seeing him, but I've never really talked to him."

"Why don't you go out with him?" Susan laughed.

"Why don't *you* go out with him?" I countered with a chuckle and a wry grin.

After the cocktail hour, we were ushered to a big round table for 10. Andrew sat next to Susan, and they chatted all evening. We ate and drank, *a lot*, and Susan and I debriefed about Andrew on the way home. We laughed about never seeing his byline anywhere, though he showed up to every free event.

"I publish all over the place, and I only make like $7,000 a year!" I said. "How does this guy possibly make a living?"

"I think he's a bookie," Susan said.

"A *what*?" I asked.

"A bookie! You know, someone who takes bets."

I shook my head. "No. I *don't* know. Never heard of it. Why do you think he's a *bookie*?"

"He talked about football a lot. He has no visible means of support but lives alone in a nice neighborhood." She paused a moment, thinking. "Yeah...so he's either a drug dealer or a bookie."

We laughed heartily. The San Diego freelance writing community was certainly full of some strange characters.

The next morning, the PR company that had put on the event the previous evening invited us to attend that night's opening as well. I was surprised when Andrew phoned and told me he'd received the same invitation and wanted to know if I was going. How had he gotten my number? I was so hungover from the night before, there was no way I could withstand another night of gastronomical onslaught. But we chatted for a bit, and I learned he'd grown up in a part of San Diego that I was writing a story about. He proposed we get together that night for coffee, and he'd tell me all about it. That was our first official date.

On our second date, Andrew invited me over to his apartment—a huge, spacious place, full of natural light, polished hardwood floors and thoughtfully furnished with vintage accents and a big, bright-yellow Naugahyde sofa. I also noticed a large, cluttered desk in the corner of his bedroom. When he excused himself to go to the bathroom, I did a quick survey of the area around his computer and noticed a pile of cash and personal checks…and I remembered Susan's words from a few nights before: "He's either a drug dealer or a bookie." *Hmm,* I thought. *Let's hope he's not a drug dealer. That's where I draw the line!*

About a week later, it all became clear and Susan looked like some kind of genius. Andrew took me to visit one of his good friends, a San Diego sportswriter named Jeff Savage and they talked openly about betting and Andrew's business, taking bets on football games and big events like the World Series for a small circle of acquaintances—by referral only. He managed to support himself by working just five months out of the year. I didn't understand any of it, but I knew it was illegal so it freaked me out a bit. When I told my mother, she was nonplussed: "Your uncle was a bookie for a while," she said. "Just be careful you don't get hauled in in a raid!"

Then came a whirlwind of outings and romantic gestures. One night, Andrew called and asked if he could bring me a hot chocolate. Another morning, I found a little plant on my porch with a note: "plant seeking pot," which followed my disappointment about selling very few of the hand-painted clay flowerpots I'd put my heart into. He was so much more thoughtful than anyone I'd ever dated. He was also a good listener and authentically cared about getting to know me.

Just weeks after we began dating, I started graduate school. As we got more serious and Andrew realized I was not the kind of woman who would marry a bookie, he put himself through a graphic design program and began working as a print and digital designer. We were both back in school at the same time, forging new professions. After I graduated in June of 1995, we eloped to Mexico in July and moved to San Francisco in August. It was a remarkable summer, and I was gleeful about a new start in a new city. I was 30 years old.

My graduate degree gave me some legitimacy to make the transition from writing to the business sector, and I needed to get a job right away. The smart thing to do would have been to work for a consulting firm, like IBM Global Services, Andersen Consulting, Accenture or KPMG—companies that hired small armies of smart, young people and placed them with their clients. Many of my classmates went this route, flying to the client site on Sunday night or early Monday morning, then back home on Friday, living in hotels during the work week. But I had just married Andrew and didn't want to be away from him.

Having a job like that for a couple of years could have provided entry to any number of corporations. A large percentage of C-suite executives get their start at consultancies like KPMG, PwC, Accenture and Ernst & Young. Had I known that when I graduated, I might have taken a different approach. Young people with corporate executives in their families know this too—another example of how family background and upbringing can propel you ahead or leave you at a disadvantage. So I floundered.

My sights were set on a corporate role at a business-to-consumer company, which abound in San Francisco. I interviewed at Gap, Levi's and Williams Sonoma, but I hadn't worked in retail stores. Gap and Levi's were looking for entry-level candidates who spent their high school and college summers folding shirts and stocking inventory. I'd worked as a restaurant server, because it paid more—I'd never considered that waiting tables would be a drawback once I started interviewing for a "real" job.

And there were some other things that ruined my chances of getting hired. When I interviewed at Gap, Andrew—now a graphic designer who collected hot sauce as a hobby—made a mini hot sauce bottle printed with the Gap logo, along with information about me. I proudly presented it to the HR person when I walked in for the interview, and I'll never forget the look of horror on her face when she saw it. It never occurred to me that I'd committed the reckless act of misappropriating Gap's logo. So I never made it past the HR screening. It wasn't until I had a few years' experience working with large companies that I realized this kind of creativity was not typically appreciated. Mega companies often have rigid corporate cultures and tend not to stray too far from the safety of their policies. It was a big miss on my part to think the hot sauce swag would make a lasting impression. Well, it did...just not the kind I was hoping for.

Discouraged and frustrated that my new degree and skills weren't opening more doors, I leaned into my personal contacts, just as I'd done when I started my freelance writing career. While I may not have looked great on paper or interviewed well, people who knew me and worked with me usually wanted to work with me again. A grad school friend who went to work for Ernst & Young started giving me freelance work, which involved creating extensive research packets on companies. I got into a good rhythm creating these reports, and the freelancing gig paid my first six months' rent out of grad school and marked my first foray into business information research.

It was 1995—the early days of digital file transfer—so I'd get a big FedEx box containing all kinds of source documents:

LexisNexis reports, SEC filings, trade magazine articles and annual reports. I'd scan through hundreds of pages, sorting and stacking them along the perimeter of our apartment, highlighting the relevant bits, tossing out the irrelevant and gradually compiling the information into a digital template. I'd deliver the final report using a dial-up modem, which took a while and was a bit harrowing when it was close to the deadline: was the file going to transfer okay, or would it crash and I'd have to start over?

My friend assigned me as many reports as I could handle, and I got faster and better at them, refining and standardizing my research methodology and process. It was a great way to earn money while I was job-hunting, but it never occurred to me to wonder what the reports were used for, or that I was gaining experience I could leverage for my career.

In the mid-1990s, there wasn't much free information available online. LexisNexis was a treasure trove, but licenses were prohibitively expensive. Ernst & Young subscribed to it, so they sent me printouts of articles—hence the piles of paper all over my apartment. Packaging the information into the template involved a lot of data entry and cutting and pasting. I wasn't creating much original content—my added value was knowing what would be useful to the client: curating a massive amount of information into what was most actionable and relevant. Eventually, I began to recognize the value of reporting and research that is not publicly available. If you can get your hands on the right info, it's like gold.

Even after accepting a full-time job in 1996, I kept my side hustle going for years. I had gotten so good at banging out those reports that it was easy money—which was helpful later, when we started a family.

In the late 1990s, tech startups were a uniquely Bay Area phenomenon. While New York City had a fledgling scene known as Silicon Alley, most of the excitement—and the money

—was coming from the peninsula that stretched between Silicon Valley and San Francisco. The media likened the Bay Area tech boom to the gold rush that built San Francisco nearly 150 years earlier. I liked to say that the dot-coms ate San Francisco. I wasn't particularly interested in technology and had no aspirations to work in the field, but that didn't matter—technology was coming for me and for everyone else in the city. No matter what you did, you were "technology-adjacent"—if you weren't making it, you were buying it, selling it, writing about it, advertising it, planning events around it or serving the people who created it. There was no escaping.

Tech ate my husband too. Andrew's background is in graphic design, and he handily made the jump to digital media, making a great living creating ad banners for all kinds of startups, including game companies. At first, the banners were static images—but before long, animation and sound were added to up the ante, the hype and, most importantly, the clicks. Andrew worked for weeks on an animated audio banner for the gaming site Pogo.com, hiring a musician friend to create the perfect *BOING* sound on a synthesizer to accompany the two "o's" in "Pogo" as they playfully bounced across the banner. For days on end, our home was filled with the sound: "*boing...boing... BOING!*" It was cutting-edge stuff at the time and very lucrative. Andrew did so much work for Pogo, we started calling our first San Francisco home "the house that Pogo built." And we needed a house now, because—while the Bay Area was giving birth to a new industry that would change the face of contemporary life— we were about to give birth to our first son.

One of the first few dozen users of Craigslist, Andrew subscribed when it was still a daily email circulated by its eponymous founder, Craig Newmark. It started as a list to keep track of all the free tech startup parties and events in San Francisco. As the tech boom grew, a few parties each week evolved into more frequent, more elaborate and more expensive extravaganzas—nearly always free to attend—and the city became a paradise of boondogglery.

Some companies hosted weekly happy hours. Once a month, a tech publication called *The Weekly Standard* held a party in its four-story brick building near North Beach. Hundreds would show up. Andrew freelanced for some of these firms, but invitations weren't required. The Bay Area also abounded with lavish tech conferences put on by big vendors like Oracle. Between the conferences, parties and regularly scheduled happy hours, you could hit multiple events every night and eat and drink (quite well) for free. As the money spent on these events escalated, each company would try to one-up the others on the party circuit.

The only thing holding us back from the all-you-can-eat-and-drink scene was our little son, who was born in November 1998. Still, about every other week, we'd hire a babysitter and venture out to a few parties. We were strategic about it, planning around the most extravagant or otherwise most promising events. We could usually squeeze in two or three, depending on the location. One legendary night, with Andrew's brother Mike and a few friends, we started at a sumptuous cocktail party held in the penthouse of the Fairmont Hotel—a mind-blowing, Moorish-style suite that has sheltered kings, presidents, rock stars and even the Kardashians—and ended the night catching the last few songs of a concert at the historic Regency Ballroom on Van Ness.

We met a lot of interesting people at these parties, and after a while, we got to know some of the players, who we'd run into all the time: thought leaders, entrepreneurs, journalists, celebrities, authors, futurists and venture capitalists. Craig Newmark of Craigslist fame was usually on the scene, and we got to know Isabel Maxwell, daughter of British media tycoon Robert Maxwell and sister of the now-infamous Ghislaine.

If you want to know the truth, I wasn't super excited about

having a baby. I felt like I had so much more to do, and the job culture wasn't what it is today. When I told people I was taking three months' leave, their responses usually were: "Wow, you're taking *a lot* of time off!" But I was 33, and it was time. I'd had a miscarriage the year before, and that made it almost a challenge for me—I'd succeed at being pregnant, damn it! And then the baby came, and I just fell in love with him. There he was: this tiny, amazing creature. I'd just stare at him all day. But I had a good book of business, so it was easy to slide back in when I was ready to go back to work.

Picture, if you will, these early days—when everyone was trying to figure out what the internet was all about and who was going to come out ahead. "Portals" to the world wide web were getting all the eyeballs and hype: Yahoo, Netscape, Ask Jeeves, MSN, Altavista, Lycos and AOL. This was pre-Google, and all everyone was talking about were portals, portals, portals. I was working downtown at DLC, a localization startup that served as a vendor to many of the well-established tech players with a presence in international markets. We translated websites, marketing materials and user interfaces into dozens of languages. I was in sales, so I was looking for companies that were expanding internationally. I knew the portal companies were going global, with bazillions of dollars to spend, and I wanted a piece of it.

I wasn't clear on what portals were, exactly, and felt like I needed to learn more, so I registered to attend a panel on "the Future of the Internet." Early in the discussion, I could have sworn I heard one panelist say "portholes" instead of "portals."

I thought, "Shit! Have I got this wrong? I've been saying, 'portals'! Oh my God, are they portholes? I've been making an idiot of myself this whole time?!"

The next thing you know, another person on the panel makes a reference to "portholes." Then it was a monkey-see, monkey-do free-for-all, with all the other chimpanzees on the panel talking about "portholes!" I could tell that some of the panelists were having the same quiet freakout I was having. You could read it on their faces: "Fuck! Is it *portals?*! Or *portholes*!?"

No longer able to stifle my giggles, I had to duck out of the session. I retreated into a bathroom stall, guffawing as silently as possible until I was gasping, tears running down my face. Was this the most dot-com story ever? I had paid to see a panel of "experts" who didn't even know if they were discussing portals or portholes. Priceless.

And I couldn't help thinking: *If these "tech-sperts" can make a go of it in the tech industry, why the hell can't I?*

CHAPTER FOUR

The Rise and Fall of Fidget

AFTER MY FIRST son was born in 1998, I decided it was time for a change. The thrill of taking Muni downtown to work every day wears off when you have a baby at home. Everyone was starting companies—why couldn't I do the same? My sister-in-law and brother-in-law had a lot of business experience, and they encouraged me to go for it, offering advice, collaborative support and even a domain name.

And so it was official: I was going into the dot-com business.

We called it Fidget. At the time, topical email newsletters supported by advertising were becoming popular. Fidget was designed to be a portal for email newsletters about a variety of topics—basically, a content and advertising company, which was a business I understood. We hired a 20-year-old programmer to build the website and crafted a whimsical logo and tagline: "Fidget: Information for Restless Minds."

Fidget's model was a digital experience—focused on a dozen original, weekly newsletters on topics like sports, investing, entertainment and cooking. Later, we added well-known syndicated content like Dear Abby, Art Buchwald, Miss Manners and other established columnists known from the print newspaper world. We delivered the newsletters via email to subscribers, so they could get all their favorite columnists in their inbox every morning. And we monetized it by wrapping the content around email advertising. This was something I easily understood, coming from magazines and being an early subscriber to email newsletters and digital content.

My sister-in-law, Lynda, encouraged me to execute what was basically her vision. She was working as an executive at Sony in LA and plotting her exit from the corporate world. She owned the Fidget.com domain and wanted to do something with it. I was thinking of leaving my sales job at DLC. Even though I had a solid book of business and was making six figures there, I liked the idea of running my own company out of my house, where I could be close to the baby. My brother-in-law Mike joined the team as CEO, Andrew did our graphic design and I hired other friends and family to do the writing. We were now a bona fide part of the dot-com scene in San Francisco.

Lynda provided $45,000 in seed money from selling some other domain names she'd owned. I knew we had to make that little bit of money last, so we tried to do as much as we could ourselves. I wore a lot of hats, handling our accounting, setting up accounts with the ad networks and writing all the web copy. The money lasted a long time—but we weren't paying ourselves anything.

Fidget was scrappy and starting to get some traction. Eventually, we were making enough to rent a small office space in San Francisco on 21st and York, in the basement of someone's home. Because of the dot-com boom, affordable commercial space was nonexistent, so a lot of homeowners were renovating and renting their garages and basements to startups.

As our subscriber base grew, we were pulling in five figures in ad revenue every month. We even got a mention in *The Wall Street Journal*. We deployed themed sweepstakes, like offering Y2K survival kits as prizes: a first-aid kit, T-shirts and lots of

Fidget-branded swag. I packaged and mailed these out myself. We hosted a sweepstakes offering a million-dollar prize with a company that pooled our user data with that of other sites. The winner was pulled from the big pool, so we weren't paying out all that much ourselves. We were getting creative and doing whatever we wanted while having a blast. The internet was still new, and a lot of money was being thrown at crazy ideas. The nascent email newsletter space showed a lot of promise, and with our momentum, we began to consider venture capital (VC) funding.

I didn't understand the VC funding model, nor had I done anything entrepreneurial before, aside from a failed attempt to sell my hand-painted flowerpots at the local flea market the summer before grad school, when I was 27. At that time, accountants and lawyers were taking on startup clients in exchange for company equity or the promise of sticking with their firms through acquisitions or IPOs, which is where they made the big money. Lynda recruited a high-powered law firm to help us mitigate risk as we navigated the startup ecosystem. They set up our ownership structure and drafted the paperwork to secure $3 million in venture capital. It was April of 2000— which marked the beginning of the historic dot-com crash— and we were pretty proud that we were pulling it off, given the timing.

To raise money, Mike and I made the rounds at VC firms, presenting our vision for Fidget. Mike and Lynda already had some exposure to VCs, so they'd make the introductions and I'd do the rest. While I understood the general concepts around term sheets and valuations, I was still learning and didn't know how to read a balance sheet or an income statement. Mike was a good coach, but I still didn't feel confident answering all the financial questions and doing the presentations. It was stressful. I felt like a snake-oil saleswoman pitching her wares from the back of a wagon in front of all these high-finance guys. While most of them were perfectly polite and treated me with respect, the teams were always 100 percent male. Having spent the previous decade working on teams led mostly by women, it felt strangely unfamiliar to be operating in all-male territory. After one meeting, I got in a cab, came home and threw up the minute I walked through the door. It turned out to be food poisoning, but it symbolized how I felt about doing investor presentations.

Another problem was that we didn't know how much to ask for. Experienced entrepreneurs tell you to raise as much as you can—even if it's more than you think you need. Our revenue model was completely advertising-based, which was starting to fall out of favor as the NASDAQ continued to plunge in the spring of 2000. This model had been the norm for the majority of the boom—everybody was selling advertising—but that model was no longer as attractive to funders. We'd done a lot with very little, pulling in at least $10,000 a month in revenue through an ad network, as well as commissions and bounties through e-commerce affiliate networks and promotions— similar to what today's influencers do on YouTube and TikTok. Our months of scaling up were paying off—both revenue and subscribers were climbing.

Fidget caught the attention of an incubator out of Burbank. For the purposes of this story, let's call it ACME because I don't want to get sued. ACME employed a bunch of ex-Disney people who had built Disney's first online presence. We were impressed by their credentials and excited about the possibility of the endorsement of these well-pedigreed digital content pioneers. It seemed a perfect match.

Mike and I flew down to Burbank to meet with their team. We hit it off, and things moved fast. Getting funded meant that ACME would take a majority stake in the company while taking over operational functions, freeing us up to focus on the core business. They'd handle HR, payroll, legal and all of the accounting—which sounded great to me, given that I was wearing all those hats with no experience in any of the disciplines. Having a majority stake also meant ACME would take a majority of seats on our board, so the new board of directors was composed of three members of ACME, plus Mike and me.

We signed the deal in April 2000 for $3 million in funding—a lump sum to be deposited upon signing, so we'd also have the benefit of interest earned—in exchange for 51 percent of the company. Then we all went up to a luxury Sonoma hotel for a couple nights for a big strategy session. After our first meeting, I privately celebrated my first foray into the world of tech. On a balcony overlooking the majestic vineyards, glass of wine in hand, I could see an expansive future that lay ahead. I'd become a genuine dot-com entrepreneur! It was one thing to start a family-run business with our own resources, but quite another to have that business validated to the tune of $3 million in venture capital. I now had a seat at the table and could participate in the conversation of the tech world as it devoured everything in its path.

With ACME's funding, we moved into a new warehouse office space at 16th and Mission in what used to be a massive butcher shop. The space was cold, cavernous and echoing—way bigger than we needed—but it was cheap and edgy and even had a basement, which had served as a meat locker back in the day. A second-floor catwalk connected offices where, we assumed, the butcher bosses used to sit—affording them privacy and the ability to survey the workers below. The space had no heat, so it was chilly in the winter, but the commercial rental market was so tight back then that we took the space anyway.

We painted the floor the bright blue of our Fidget logo, moved in our iMacs and Ikea desks and began hiring. We ordered all kinds of Fidget swag and stocked the kitchen with beer, wine and snacks. We signed a year-long server hosting contract as well as other long-term contracts we needed to grow the business. With a staff of ten in place, Mike and I finally started paying ourselves. It wasn't as much as I was making at DLC, but I was elated to be paid a decent salary for doing my own thing. And we'd managed all this amidst the dot-com crash.

While Fidget was on the rise, most of Andrew's ad banner work dried up as that boom began to go bust. With a young family to support, Andrew refocused his banner business on a more reliable source of income, in the oldest industry in the world. He managed to get a gig producing ad banners for online purveyors of porn and sex toys. Now that the online ad business had reached a certain level of maturity and measurability, marketers were focused on improving ad performance, endlessly tweaking the images and fiddling with messaging to eke out a few more percentage points of clicks or sales.

Andrew worked from home and had one full-time employee —a quiet, mild-mannered youngster named Lawrence—whom he was trying to retain, despite the downturn. We also had our nanny, Lydia, in the house on a daily basis to help us with our newborn.

One morning, I was making coffee in the kitchen, which was adjacent to Andrew's office, when Lydia came in.

"I got him down for a nap."

"Oh my God, you're a magician. Want some coffee?"

"Sure."

Andrew was conducting a client meeting on speakerphone in the next room, and we couldn't avoid hearing:

"The butt-plug ad was our top performer. Should we do some more versions and schedule those for next month?"

"What are you envisioning there? Different-colored plugs, tighter on the anus?"

Lawrence's desk was right next to the kitchen, his large monitor all too visible. Lydia spent much of her time prepping bottles and washing dishes—and God love her, she never said a word about the oiled-up, half-naked men Lawrence meticulously manipulated on his monitor all day as he created banner after banner for a gay porn site.

I'm sure she had questions—and a lot to talk about with her friends and family after work. But in the one-industry town that San Francisco had become, even the nannies knew what was up. They could see as well as anybody that the deep well of venture capital had run dry and the layoffs were piling up. So we were all grateful that the money was still flowing in our house—fortunate indeed to be on solid ground, with tech stocks in freefall and dot-com startups imploding all around us. In fact, I was so confident, I booked a two-week trip to Italy, to take place in November.

Before I left on vacation, we got news that ACME had hired a new CEO with a biotech background. Soon after, we were told the ACME board was engineering a major pivot of its portfolio—away from content companies to biotech. The Disney folks—who were probably as nervous as we were—told us we needed to devise a new business plan. Somehow, they didn't seem as friendly as before...but we were encouraged that the firm hadn't let them go despite the change in focus.

Obviously, we couldn't pivot to biotech—it was too major a shift—but we thought we'd be safe as long as the Disney guys were still there. While this wasn't an ideal situation, we were on solid ground: they were contractually obligated to fund the $3 million—the deal had been signed months earlier. With the change in direction, we knew they likely wouldn't fund us for another round, so we planned to use the investment to build a viable business, then go from there. We also knew we weren't alone—they'd funded other consumer content companies—so we hoped they'd keep the team of ex-Disney guys to manage the content portfolio they'd already committed to funding. It was the best we could hope for.

We expected the Disney guys to be our allies, and they were —up until the day they weren't.

When I returned from vacation in November, Mike and I had two weeks to come up with a new business plan, but there was one major problem: we were at a loss at how to create more revenue beyond advertising. What else can you do with newsletters? People weren't paying for content in 2000. But we worked diligently on a new plan, the focus of which was more aggressive revenue growth. Mike and I gathered our final thoughts on the pitch we'd lead with when the board meeting opened, and we dialed in to the teleconferencing number for the quarterly meeting.

We started the call with the usual niceties. "Hello, how are you doing? Good? That's great."

The ACME board members brought the meeting to order, but before Mike and I could launch into our presentation for the new business plan—or even speak—they immediately called for a vote:

"All those in favor of dissolving Fidget today, say aye."

"Aye."

"Aye."

"Aye."

The three ACME board members voted in favor. There was only Mike and me left. They had the majority vote, the majority of seats on the board, the majority of our stock.

Stunned, Mike and I voted: our "nays" weak and puny as it dawned on us what had happened. It was done. Fidget was done. We'd been utterly blindsided. There'd been no mention of a new business plan—it was all a ruse.

In shock, we hung up and sat silently, looking at one another. My heart was beating in my chest, but I had no words.

Then there was a knock at the front door, and a process server handed us each an envelope. *What the fuck was this now?* We opened the envelopes to learn that ACME was *suing us for fraud!* To add insult to injury, the note on the process server's envelopes described Mike as "pudgy" and me as "fortyish." I was only 35!

We'd known the outlook for Fidget was not good, but never did we imagine something like this. Mike and I had never fully trusted the "money people," as we called them, but we were astounded by ACME's shameless chicanery: the board meeting scheduled under false pretenses. The red herring of the new business plan. The vote to dissolve the company with no discussion. And finally, the lawsuit to scare us into backing down from a fight. Purely devious.

In retrospect, Mike and I should have been more prepared, but—silly us—we thought we were protected by a signed contract for the funding commitment. But the funds were in an account ACME controlled—because, as an incubator, they'd taken over the handling of our finances. Beware the incubator: it sounds great to an entrepreneur not to have to manage payroll and track benefits and all of that, but their control over our accounts made it that much easier to shut us down. Later, we found out that they had never put the full $3 million in our bank account—a blatant breach of contract that also deprived us of six months of interest the money would have earned.

Next was the hardest part. We gathered our employees and told them the news. We were honest and direct. Our main contact at ACME was coming to the office in a couple of hours to speak with Mike and me, so everyone stuck around to see what would happen. We didn't know what to expect—would they remove everything from the office? Would they offer severance payments? We wanted our employees to get out with as much as they could. Mike and I had used Lynda's seed money to pay for office supplies, furniture and computers, so we instructed everyone to pack up their cars with whatever we had paid for ourselves. We knew we were all about to be fired, but ACME didn't have an inventory of our office supplies, and we'd be damned if we were going to give them what belonged to us. We took everything that wasn't nailed down.

I was red-hot pissed. The ACME guy coming to see us had been one of our supposed champions. He was a nice guy, but when he walked in, I looked at him as if my eyes could shoot bullets. The three of us walked upstairs to the enclosed catwalk. We didn't even sit down—we just stood facing each other. I was hostile—after all, they were suing us for fraud. Mike was more pragmatic and businesslike, calmly asking questions about severance and the funding.

Then came the kicker. The Disney guy offered Mike and me a choice: we could each receive $100,000, or we would get *nothing*, and our employees would receive severance. What I heard was, "We'll give you each a chunk of money if you're willing to screw over your employees."

Mike and I could see everyone down below, watching us. We didn't even leave the room to discuss it privately—we both knew the right answer. We chose severance for all of Fidget's employees. Everyone would get three weeks' salary.

After the ACME guy left, Mike and I shared the news with the team. Even though we knew what the outcome was going to be, we were all in shock. Within a half hour, everyone's cars were packed up with most of Fidget's office. Then we went out for drinks.

The next day we met with Leor, our lawyer, and showed him the papers we'd been served. ACME was accusing us of fraudulently misrepresenting our revenue—a tactic to try and get out of the $3 million commitment. Leor agreed that ACME was in breach of contract and we had every right to countersue. We could prove that they never fully funded us, and we could disprove their accusation of fraud.

But he warned us, "You can sue the shit out of them, but it's going to be awful and you're going to spend all your money on lawyers." He proposed that we negotiate a settlement, and in the end we agreed on $400,000 and retained ownership of the domain name. While we wouldn't get the justice we deserved, Leor had given us good advice. I was eight weeks pregnant with our second son, and I had no intention of spending the next few months in a lawsuit. He said he'd seldom seen a funder pull something so nasty and sleazy. He could tell by their tactics that they were determined to get out of the deal and were prepared to fight dirty to do it.

So I spent the next six months shutting Fidget down. The sad irony was that the month Fidget was dissolved, we brought in our highest earnings yet, with more than $40,000 in ad revenue. That money went straight to us, and I used it to pay our vendors as much as I could, as well as paying myself $2,000 a month for the unpleasant work of winding down my dream.

As for the ex-Disney guys who brought us in to ACME, they must have known they were circling the drain as well. As the economic situation worsened, ACME cut jobs and pivoted to patent trolling—going after porn sites to collect bounties for patent infringement. When the economy gets tough, people show their true colors. The experience made me exceedingly cautious about who I got into bed with later. If I ever ran a business again, I'd know better than to turn over majority control to another party.

Weeks afterward, I'd lie in bed crying and beating the mattress with my fists. It was the only outlet I had for my rage after getting royally screwed by ACME. But on the bright side, I was looking forward to the birth of my second son, which would come as a joyful and welcome relief.

CHAPTER FIVE

Is That a Polenta in Your Pocket?

WITH FIDGET GONE and Andrew riding the fumes of the tech crash, I had to find a job that would pay well enough to cover our expenses and the cost of a nanny for our kids. We'd moved into a new house two weeks before our second son was born—just days before the real estate market took a temporary dip. We paid top dollar at the height of the market, and our new mortgage was double that of our last house. Fidget's implosion was so scary, we considered paying a kill fee to back out of buying the new house, but because of the market dip, everybody threw in some money to save the deal—our realtors relinquished some of their commission, and the owner cut the price by four-and-a-half percent. They knew that if the house went back on the market, it wouldn't sell amidst a crash that was turning out to be bigger and more sustained than anyone anticipated.

It was June 2001—everyone in San Francisco was feeling the impact of rampant layoffs. When my mom came to help me unpack, she was bewildered by the nonstop stream of friends stopping by throughout what would normally be the workday, to bring food, hang out and help us unpack.

"Doesn't *anyone* have a *job* around here?"

"Actually…no, they don't," I replied.

Few were panicking...yet. Most people had been working hard, making big salaries and collecting stock options between 1997 and 2000. While many of those options were now worthless, they'd put some money away and were happy to have a break. Unemployed friends took time to travel, work on pet projects and start a family or engineer a career pivot into nonprofits or academia.

It was an interesting time to live in the city. San Francisco is fueled by irrational exuberance—from the gold rush to the tech boom, you just ride the wave as it roars in, crests, then dissipates. Opportunists flock to the city and take up all the restaurant reservations, crowd the parks, clog the streets and throw their money around. Those of us who have ridden multiple waves of booms and busts have experienced the city at its worst —frenetic, out of balance and unsustainable. Our famously eccentric, permissive and laid-back town—which at seven square miles is typically easy to navigate—becomes a hot, angry cauldron about to boil over. The streets get a whole lot meaner.

During the height of the first dot-com bubble in 1999, a friend witnessed a driver, trapped in an epic traffic jam, standing up through his sunroof so he could scream obscenities and heave a bottle of Snapple at another car. During the most recent bubble, another friend saw a young couple ridiculing a homeless man in a wheelchair. They clutched each other and snickered as he tried again and again to navigate a curb—the chair piled high with his belongings. They even filmed him so they could post his misery for the enjoyment of fellow assholes.

This is the kind of stuff you see when the city becomes inundated with fortune seekers who don't buy into the San Francisco ethos. They care little for the community. And just when it seems like things can't get more toxic, everything crashes: the speculators move out and the city feels calm and manageable again—like it's been washed clean by a hard rain. In my three decades in San Francisco, I've survived multiple boom-bust cycles and witnessed the upside of the downturns, where the city becomes livable again, and those of us who remain can slow down and breathe.

We were dealt a one-two punch when the dot-com crash of 2000 was followed by 9/11. The options for going back to work seemed even more limited, and Andrew's ad banner work had dried up almost entirely. Even though I now had some solid business experience, I didn't think I could afford to be strategic or choosy—we had two little kids and a great big mortgage. As the primary breadwinner, I didn't have the luxury of taking six months to look around. I liked the pace of sales and tech-adjacent marketing, and I'd run my own company, but out-of-work people like me were a dime a dozen.

So I wondered if it was time to do something completely different. I was interested in the high-end retail food space and interviewed at a couple of local gourmet markets—but the pay was low and would barely cover the cost of childcare, let alone the mortgage. Fun, but not remotely realistic. Then I saw an ad on Craigslist for a sales job at a company that tested and rated foods and appliances—which could offer exposure to a new industry in a way that had more earning potential.

The company was headquartered downtown in a real dump of a building. *Not a great sign*, I thought, as I sat in the dingy lobby. But things started to look up when an elegant, handsome man came to fetch me for the interview. Well-spoken, with a voice made for radio, Tom Allen was in his mid-50s, and rumor had it that he owned the biggest house in Half Moon Bay.

Tom's candor took me by surprise when he explained he was in the process of transforming the business—rebranding and implementing a legitimate business model due to the shady reputation the company had earned under former leadership— which is why he needed credible people, like me. I should have walked out then, but I didn't. I was intrigued. I found his honesty refreshing. And hey, it certainly wouldn't be dull. But mainly...I had no other options.

A panel of foodies from around the city was paid to taste and rank food products or test small appliances and kitchen tools. We're talking corn flakes, ketchups, coffee makers and cheese graters—pretty much anything you might find in your kitchen. Products were rated on various criteria, and a winner designated in each category. My job was to contact the manufacturers prior to each competition and get them to send in their products for free. When the judging was complete, I'd call the winners, letting them know their products had won, and offer the rights to use our award on their packaging. Nice, right? For a price...Then I'd negotiate a licensing deal, usually around $15,000 a year. Small change for such notoriety...particularly among big brands that probably spent that much in petty cash on a daily basis.

Prior to Tom's revamping of the business model, the winners had 48 hours to decide whether they wanted to purchase the rights. If they turned it down, the award was offered to the runner-up: always, by nature of the beast, a competitor. The math was easy to do from a marketing perspective—paying the piper to prevent your competition from claiming the award was the smartest answer to that equation.

The math on our side was a no-brainer as well: $15,000, multiplied by every major brand in every possible category— annually—added up to mountains of money for this relatively lean, boiler-room operation. The more categories we judged, the more money we made—so instead of one award for the best mozzarella, they sliced and diced the category into as many slivers as they could: shredded mozzarella, mozzarella sticks, whole milk mozzarella, skim milk mozzarella, organic mozzarella, vegan mozzarella and on and on. Complete horseshit or ingenious business model? Either way, we'd earned a reputation among competitors, and it wasn't a good one.

I started out all in, confident I could help Tom reposition the program as legit. My strategy was to establish credibility and build trust with the brand managers. I had forged solid customer relationships when I was in sales at DLC, so I was confident I'd be able to do the same here. So…after composing a loose script to work from, I made my first call to one of the big household name brands. I'd barely uttered the name of our company before I received a hot "Fuck you!" and the person on the other end slammed down the phone. I'm not exaggerating—these brand managers *hated* us. This was going to be a lot harder than I thought.

The first person who agreed to have an actual conversation with me was from Kellogg's. As I began my pitch about our new and improved program, she interrupted me and said, "Yeah, I know you guys—if we don't pay, you'll offer it to a competitor."

I proudly shared the news of the changes we'd made to make the program legit: "If you don't take the award, your competitor cannot take it. The category will go dormant for a year, and no one else can claim it."

Silence.

"Wait a minute," she said, "if we don't pay, you're not gonna offer it to anyone else?"

I confirmed that we wouldn't.

Delighted, she replied, "That's great! Well then…we'll pass!"

And so it went with nearly every call I made. Our revenue plunged under the integrity of the new business model. And as Tom Allen and I fought to clear our name and earn the company a new reputation, it was business as usual for the legacy salespeople, who'd been cleaning up in quite another way. My sales manager, whom I'll call Dick, was making hundreds of thousands in commissions. He wasn't about to change the MO. His second-in-command, a woman I'll call Joan, despised me from day one—she must have sensed my earnestness and honesty. Her style was to undermine and sabotage me from the shadows, and she and Dick fought tooth and nail to preserve the status quo.

Come to find out, Dick and Joan regularly rigged the process to favor companies they knew were willing to pay the licensing fee—usually with products so bad they needed a seal on their box to trick people into buying them. For example, Joan made sure a shitty drug-store chocolate company with whom she had a long relationship won the award for boxed, filled chocolates every single year. The brand was mediocre crap, but the judges kept choosing it as the winner, year after year. The judging was always blind, so I couldn't figure out why these crappy chocolates always won. I later found out that Joan was taking the competitor's chocolates home on the weekends, alternating them between the hot sun and her freezer until they developed an unappetizing white film on the surface. I also heard her admit that she spritzed some items with hairspray.

This kind of behavior wasn't hidden. In fact, it was bragged about and encouraged among the sales team. And corruption and backstabbing were part of the culture. I had never experienced anything like it. People thought nothing of stealing from the company and each other. When the competitions branched out into booze categories, Joan walked out of the office with a case of Tanqueray that had been sent to me for my upcoming gin tasting, forcing me to run out to a liquor store to buy replacements.

I shared a sad little office with a guy from Brooklyn named Angelo—an investment manager and would-be-entrepreneur who'd been on the verge of launching his own company before 9/11. His idea revolved around the airlines, and he'd lined up deals with all the major players—but after 9/11, they all pulled out. When he accepted the job with Tom Allen, he was two weeks away from being homeless.

Angelo and I had little in common—he was an East Coast "guy's guy"—but because we were hired around the same time, we developed a tight bond, forged over nothing more than how fucking crazy this place was. As his office mate, I listened to sales calls as Angelo earnestly described to a brand manager how carefully we would evaluate their mozzarella sticks and shredded cheese in a Brooklyn accent I was used to hearing only from tough guys in the movies. My suppressed giggles often escalated into waves of full-fledged hysteria, especially if dissed by a prospective competitor, when he'd slam down the phone and yell, "Well, fuck you too, you friggin' *asshole!*" Brooklyn style. We lampooned each other incessantly, and for such a miserable job, I've never laughed so much in my life.

One day, Angelo left his credit card on his desk when he went to lunch, and Joan snatched it right up and used it all weekend to pay for cab fare, expensive dinners and drinks. No one could make this stuff up. It was as grim and as viciously backbiting as *Glengarry Glen Ross*. I couldn't believe this was my life.

I personally organized five competitions every week, so I had to cold-call at least six companies two or three times a week per competition, to ask them to send their products in. Some ignored my calls and never sent anything, which meant I'd have to go out and buy the stuff. I tried my best to convince them that we were legit under our new owner. I eventually made some headway: I'd managed to convince about half the companies I called to send their stuff to us, but I'd have to go out to buy the other half. Angelo and I were relieved to get away from the insanity of the office and spent as much time as we could driving around the city shopping.

The company had a strict rule that we each had to make at least 60 calls a day. They even had a call-counting machine hooked up to an ancient dot-matrix printer, which buzzed to life every time a call was made, logging the phone number and the initiator of the call. Every morning, Dick the sales manager awaited our arrival with our call numbers in hand. And every morning, he confronted me, saying I wasn't making enough calls.

"Listen, Dick. There's no good reason to make 60 calls a day —my products are coming in!"

"Sixty calls *per*, Sharon—that's the rule."

I threw up my hands. "Who else do you want me to call? Do you want me to be a pest and call everyone ten times a week? Dick, do the math. No one needs to make that many calls."

Yet every day, there'd be a printout of the call report sitting on our chairs, listing everyone's name and how many calls they made. Invariably, Joan was at the top of the list, with over 90 calls a day.

Angelo and I were bewildered by their obsession with the call report. It just didn't add up—we couldn't possibly make any more calls without harassing our contacts. To pad his numbers, Angelo called his mom several times a day until she demanded that he stop calling her.

"Even my own mother doesn't wanna talk to me! Who am I gonna call now?"

We were desperate to boost our call numbers. I'd call my friends, my husband, my mom—anyone I could think of. But our people were growing sick of hearing from us; we were becoming pariahs with our own family and friends.

I finally noticed the call report was showing fewer calls than I was actually making. Something was off. I started tracking my calls on Post-it notes. Sure enough, the number of calls on my report was always a lot lower. I did some digging and found the original call reports in a stack on Dick's desk. It was pretty obvious that someone had cut out the call numbers next to my name and replaced them with a lower number. It had been done with such painstaking detail that it was unnoticeable on the copies that were circulated to the sales team. And I noticed something else on the original report...and that's when I plotted my revenge.

One day, when Dick wouldn't cease harping on my call numbers, I stormed out of his office and made a beeline to the end of the hall, where the heinous call machine was noisily spitting out its report. I ripped out the long sheet of paper and marched back into his office.

"Here! Look at that, right there. And that. And that. Keep going!"

I pointed at the list of Joan's calls. Almost all of them were to one number: the Time Lady. Okay, I'm dating myself now, but here goes: Pre-2007, there was a number you could call from any area code—the number spelled POPCORN—and a computerized female voice (known as the Time Lady) would recite the accurate time. In pre-internet days, if there was a power outage and you needed to reset your clock, the Time Lady was the best way to get the accurate time.

I tapped my forefinger on the call log repeatedly. "Notice anything…repetitive, Dick? Notice any bullshit here?"

Joan was calling the Time Lady about 50 times a day.

I stormed out of his office, and he never harassed me—or anyone else—about call numbers ever again.

Angelo called me his hero.

Amazingly, as 2002 arrived, things got even worse. Tom Allen had a personal driver who also happened to be a professional mime. He was six foot five, fully bald, and had an intimidating presence and a booming tenor voice. He told jokes to Tom as he drove him around San Francisco, which apparently charmed Tom so much, he hired the mime-chauffeur as vice president of the company.

Having no idea what he was supposed to be doing, this hulking clown seemed to think the job involved lumbering around the office, sexually harassing all the women. It was the unfortunate era of low-riding pants, and—like every other woman in America brainwashed by fashion—I was doing my best to make this look work for me, despite not having the body for it. In my defense, it wasn't like I had much choice. For a while, it was the only style the stores were selling.

The mime-driver-cum-vice president loved this look and thought it was fun to sneak up behind the women in the office to peek at our underwear down the back of our gaping, low pant waists.

"Nice underwear today, Sharon. Is that pink or mauve?" he'd say after slithering up behind me as I sat at my desk.

"Fuck off, asshole!" As a 37-year-old woman who'd experienced her share of sexual harassment, I didn't skip a beat. "Now get the hell out of my office."

Angelo guffawed. "Atta girl. You went all Brooklyn on him!"

Most women my age viewed sexual harassment as something that came with the territory if you wanted to have a career, and I'd grown a thick skin about the things men do and say in the workplace.

One week, the company was evaluating national brands of polenta, some of which were packaged into tubular rolls, à la Jimmy Dean pork sausage. I was sitting at my desk, killing time —enjoying a cup of coffee and fantasizing about quitting my job —when in walks the mime-chauffeur, proudly presenting himself as he unzipped his pants, reached in and pulled out a two-pound roll of polenta, playfully wagging it in my face.

That night, after I put the kids down, I detailed the day's madness for Andrew, and while we both had a good laugh about the mime and his polenta penis, we knew something had to give. He encouraged me to quit, but we needed the money and health insurance the job provided. The job market in San Francisco was still in a ditch, and it would be difficult to get another job. But the polenta incident was the final straw.

When I saw Angelo the next morning, I told him I was quitting.

His eyes lit up. "*Do* it, *do* it!" He was thrilled that one of us would break free.

I sat at my desk, unsure of what to do next. "I really want to quit, but now I'm more nervous than pissed. I don't know if I have the guts to do it today."

Angelo reached into his desk drawer, pulled out a little container and handed me a pill. "Take one of these," he said. "I use it for my panic attacks."

It was a Xanax.

"I don't want to be too drugged up."

"Then just take half. You can take the rest later—to celebrate!"

I thought about it, shrugged, then bit off half and put the rest in the coin pocket of my wallet.

About a half hour later, I glided into Tom Allen's office. It was my best quit ever.

"Tom, I understand you want to legitimize this place. I know exactly what you need to do, and I have repeatedly told you what steps we need to take. But none of it has happened. Your legacy salespeople are still doing things the old way, and you're not holding them accountable, which sabotages the rest of us. There's nothing more I can do to help you, so I'm resigning."

He gave me a long look. "Wow. Okay."

It was probably the first time I had his full attention. He asked me what I thought he should do to make the company better, and I told him, step by step. The Xanax had made me delightfully calm, confident and clear headed. Plus I had not a single fuck left to give.

"And about your new vice president—"

He froze for about a split second, then cut me off. "Well, you know, Sharon, we've been wanting to launch a nice glossy magazine about food-product innovation and the work we do with our judges. Would you be willing to be editor-in-chief on a contract basis?"

I blinked. "Yes, I would. For a fee of $10,000."

He nodded slowly. "Okay, let's draw up the papers. I'm really sorry you're going to be leaving, but I'm glad you'll still be working for us."

Hot damn! I'd walked into Tom's office to quit and walked out with a $10,000 consulting gig to tie me over financially until I could figure things out. Best of all, I could consult from home and would never have to set foot in that godforsaken place ever again.

I was delighted.

I went back to my desk, put my head down and fell into a blissful, Xanax-induced nap.

My timing to leave turned out to be fortuitous: a group of several young women filed a sexual harassment lawsuit against the company because of the antics of the mime-chauffeur-vice president. They asked if I wanted to join the suit, but I declined. I had never complained to company management about the mime's unwanted attention or given them an opportunity to address the problem, so I didn't feel I had the right to sue. Suing also seemed like a long, drawn-out hassle that would only distract and weigh me down. I wanted to move on. For decades, I'd handled these incidents outside of HR and the legal system—why should this time be any different? At age 37, I had a great set of tools for fending off sexual harassers. My tactics were consistently effective: once I told someone off, they usually didn't mess with me again. I've been told that when I get fully angry, I am absolutely terrifying. I don't see it myself, but who am I to argue with such consistent feedback?

The lawsuit did come into play later—about the time I'd finished the magazine project for Tom Allen. The first issue had gone to press, and it was beautiful. But as the weeks went by and I hadn't received a penny of my $10,000 fee, I worried that I was going to get stiffed. I called Tom nearly every day about the payment, but he wasn't returning my calls. Then I received a phone call from a lawyer the company had retained to defend them in the sexual harassment suit. He asked if I'd ever seen the mime-chauffeur do anything inappropriate.

I matter-of-factly replied: "Yes, actually. One day he came into my office and pulled a two-pound cylinder of polenta out of his pants and waved it in my face, like it was his penis."

The attorney paused for a very long time. "Have you been contacted by the plaintiff's lawyer?" he asked.

I declined to say.

He was about to ask another question, but I was out of patience and cut him off. "Look—your client owes me 10 grand for work I just completed, and they're not paying me or returning my calls—so at this point, I'm weighing all my options. But, for the record, I will reiterate: he waved a roll of polenta in my face like it was his dick."

The check arrived via FedEx the very next day. I howled with laughter as I opened that envelope, imagining the attorney calling Tom Allen, screaming: "Are you out of your fucking mind? *Pay that woman now!*"

I felt like a 24-karat badass. I couldn't wait to share my story with my Aunt Betty, the corporate CFO. She'd seen a lot in her day, but I was pretty confident no one had ever pulled a polenta out of his pants for her benefit.

It was 2002. After this absurd six-month career detour, I was determined never to work for anybody ever again. As always, my lack of strategic planning in my career path was my biggest weakness. But in hindsight, I can see how everything was leading me in one direction: the startup experience with Fidget, the worst job I've ever had and even my Baskin-Robbins and waitressing jobs led to my being crazy-determined to get what I wanted. Those jobs burned a belief into me that if I wanted good things to happen, I'd have to make them happen myself. I also knew I could survive any work situation, no matter how toxic, with my integrity, ambition and good humor intact.

But I was once again out of work and didn't know what to do next. I had to start networking.

CHAPTER SIX

From Spaghetti Sauce to Tech Marketing

I DON'T LIKE ASKING for help, and I'm not good at staying in touch with everyone all the time. And I never want to be the person who reaches out only to ask for something. It was hard for me, but I sent a Hail Mary mass email to everyone I knew. I was in survival mode.

And the replies flooded in. I was bowled over by people's generosity and helpfulness, even those I didn't know very well. I got several small writing jobs right away and had lots of conversations that didn't pan out but did lead to more referrals. It taught me that most people want to help, and it's something I always try to remember and pay forward. Even if I haven't heard from them in forever, I am always happy to engage.

My first freelance job was for Andrew's friend Dave, who had a successful gourmet food products business. He did private-label work making sauces for brands like Williams Sonoma. His wife normally cooked up his samples in their home kitchen, but she was very pregnant and couldn't do it this time, so he asked me if I'd be willing. He gave me the recipes to make jumbo batches of three different sauces. I did all the shopping and made the sauces, ladling them into jars I'd sterilized in the dishwasher. I was paid 200 bucks for a huge amount of work, but it was fun and it felt good to be earning money on my own.

Then I heard from a former colleague named Paolo, who'd been my sales assistant at DLC, the localization company. Paolo and I worked great together. He was super smart, ambitious and had more natural business acumen than I did. He came from an educated family, and his father was a diplomat. When we put pitches together for potential clients, he'd read everything about the company he could get his hands on, which took a lot of time —often more than we had. Ironically, at the time I considered such background research overkill. He tried to explain, "We need to understand their strategy." My boss at DLC told me the same thing, recommending I read all our customers' and prospects' annual reports—and while I gamely complied, I honestly didn't get it. *Really?* I thought. *We're just selling 'em translations!* I didn't yet understand the importance of business intelligence.

After I left DLC to have babies, took my entrepreneurial detour with Fidget and worked at the crazy-ass food judging place, I could see that I'd wasted a lot of time with my arbitrary and reactive career choices. Paolo, on the other hand, was flying high after leaving DLC. He'd joined an event marketing agency called Carlson Marketing, whose parent company owned Howard Johnson's and TGI Fridays. He quickly became a super-star there, supporting their business of staging huge events for tech companies like Intel. When he saw my email asking for help, he brought me in for a meeting with his boss—they were looking for some new thinking around Intel's event strategy and wanted to hear my thoughts. I was excited but also terrified; I didn't know anything about Intel, tech companies or events!

Paolo waved away my concerns. "You're perfect for this!" he said.

I can't remember what happened at that meeting, but I'm certain I did not say anything particularly brilliant.

Nonetheless, Paolo's boss said my presentation was the best he'd ever seen. I hadn't presented a damn thing! To this day, I'm certain he had me confused with someone else. But I took the win and was greenlighted as their newest marketing strategy consultant.

Carlson brought me in to work on the Intel strategy, which led to more projects. As Paolo and I brainstormed, I felt pressure to make him look good. The stakes were high, both in terms of not letting him down and finally launching myself into a sustainable new career I wasn't embarrassed to discuss with friends and family (like my last gig). It was stressful and scary, but soon—with Paolo's guidance—I was confidently running with any task he gave me.

When Paolo moved to another agency, he took me with him. The transition quickly built up my network and credibility in the tech-marketing community, but I was still on shaky ground —suffering from imposter syndrome. I couldn't shake the nagging feeling that I didn't really know what I was doing. And after what happened with Fidget, I was terrified I'd get crushed in the male-dominated field of big tech.

Whenever Paolo and I crafted a presentation, I'd build the PowerPoint strategy deck—which required becoming fluent in both client-specific and industry-specific jargon. It was a little like learning a new language. I remember the first time I heard a fellow consultant use the term "go to market." It sounded ridiculous, and I couldn't stop thinking about the Mother Goose "This Little Piggy" nursery rhyme, the only other place I'd ever heard the phrase. Who made this stuff up, anyway? There was so much to learn, it was like drinking from a firehose. I was acutely aware and fearful that revealing my lack of jargon knowledge would expose me as the imposter I was. Fortunately,

I managed to hold my own, and with each meeting, clients wanted more. And more. Paolo and I had become a dynamic team.

In tech marketing, almost every document is produced in PowerPoint—each meeting agenda, meeting notes, every list— all recorded and nicely formatted as slide decks, as if they would be presented to the CEO. I often delivered the same presentations to multiple groups throughout a client's company. This was called "socializing" the material. I was baffled (and delighted) I was getting paid to present the same material over and over again—sometimes for months or even a whole year! In addition to the financial benefit, it helped me refine and improve my presentations: hearing the types of questions that would come up, I learned to field them like an expert.

The principle of "defensibility" I'd learned from Ginny at *San Diego Magazine* decades earlier made my research rock solid and became a touchstone of my methodology as a presenter. I revised my decks to proactively address any issues that might prompt questions or objections, and incorporate feedback— relishing the challenge, scanning my audience to try to predict who might give me a hard time. "Bring it on motherfucker!" I'd think to myself. I saw firsthand that people liked my work, and I became an unflappable presenter. With every successful project, my confidence got another boost, motivating me to keep going.

Working with Paolo resulted in a very lucrative and exciting six years. In that time, he moved to four different companies in progressively more senior roles and brought me in to consult with clients like PeopleSoft, Oracle, Cisco, IBM, Google, Adobe, AMD and VMware—nearly all of the biggest tech companies in the Bay Area. I got through the "fake it 'til you make it" stretch, and it wasn't long before I was a bona fide expert in my new field, earning a great living.

Meanwhile, Andrew was flourishing on the home front. The

consummate stay-at-home dad, he loved nothing more than shuttling our sons to and from school, playdates, the neighborhood parks—happily handling everything from the shopping to the childrearing. We couldn't have been a more compatible pair for all our differences in that area. I didn't possess the natural facility Andrew had for parenting and socializing. The more kids he had around him, the happier he was. Ours was the house all the kids flocked to for fun and good times—provided I wasn't at home! I loved my kids, but I just didn't have the comfort level with other people's children and all the running around and constant activity...My forte was in the world of business, so Andrew's gifts were a blessing to us both.

When the kids were starting grammar school, Andrew wanted to buy a Volvo wagon—the kind with the jump seat in the rear so he could pile even more children into our car. "No way in hell," I said. But Andrew put his foot down on that one, and when I heard him whispering on the phone about the car one day, I knew it was a fait accompli. He picked his battles wisely and dug in his heels only about once a year—on matters that were dear to his heart—and our new Volvo wagon was a testament to the joy he felt from being the best dad ever.

Meanwhile, I continued to follow Paolo as he moved on to some of the bigger global event marketers, including George P. Johnson and Freeman Co., who ran corporate marketing events and trade shows all over the world. Some were huge, global events for corporations like Oracle OpenWorld and Salesforce Dreamforce, attracting more than 40,000 in-person attendees.

In the late 1990s and early 2000s, purchasing enterprise-wide technology was still the domain of mid-level management. Salespeople would contact managers via cold call or generic email, or meet them at tradeshows. So the tradeshow business was going gangbusters, and one of my first jobs was to assemble event portfolios for companies like Cisco: I helped figure out which of the hundreds of tradeshows around the world they should attend or sponsor—looking into the demographics of the attendees, the content and the sponsorship packages—and come back with recommendations of the 50 or so events that would be wise investments in terms of potential enterprise-wide sales.

The internet boom changed the tech industry's sales paradigm dramatically: it gave buyers the ability to do more of their pre-purchase research online, rather than having sales meetings with vendors. It came down to the fact that buyers didn't want to be sold to anymore. Consequently, industry events focused on education and relationship-building rather than the sales process. Customers who purchased a vendor's tech attended an event to troubleshoot specific problems they were having or anticipating, or to secure executive facetime to ensure a vendor's commitment to their needs.

Other conferences were more intimate, high-end affairs for just a few hundred, or even a few dozen, senior executives from Fortune 500 companies. The smaller events were held at exclu-sive resorts, in places like Kiawah Island off the coast of South Carolina, or Pebble Beach in Monterey, with golf, tennis, skiing, sailing and, of course, networking. Our clients were tech companies looking to spend quality relationship-building time with Fortune 500 C-suite executives, to market directly to that level of senior leadership, bypassing midlevel management.

Around this time, decisions on company-wide tech—like a customer relationship management (CRM) tool (products like Salesforce or NetSuite) that impacts all levels of an organization —were becoming more heavily influenced by C-level manage-ment. If a chief revenue officer knows its company needs a new CRM to sustain future growth, they'd issue a request for proposals (RFP) to a short list of vendors. So unless they had an inside scoop, tech vendors had to wait until an RFP was issued before they knew there was an opportunity for a big deal. Aside from cold-calling, there was no way to proactively approach C-level execs to sell them on big-ticket, enterprise-wide licenses. And my customers began to wonder how they might gain a competitive edge by "getting ahead of the RFP."

The simplest strategy for marketers was to lock and load an email campaign, set to go out over the next six months, known as the "spray-and-pray" method. But the results were often counter to what the team was trying to achieve. And even if an email got the attention of a midlevel, the C-level folks still had to be engaged because the deals are huge—sometimes as high as nine figures—and the tech is transformative, touching all parts of the company.

I could see a variety of marketing strategies starting to unfold back in the mid-2000s: from granularly focused, account-based marketing strategies to lock-and-load email sprays—each of which had its up- and downsides. In keeping with the change ushered in by the internet era, the tech industry was now riding the wave it had created—struggling to stay upright on its own board. And as I watched some crash into the water before the wave even crested while others sailed to shore, one thing was certain: C-level executive engagement was going to be crucial, and I wanted to help my customers crack the code. I decided to reposition my consulting around this specific challenge.

One such surfer was Scott McNealy, CEO of Sun Microsystems. Around 2005, Scott was called upon to assist Sun's sales effort targeting its top 200 must-win accounts. His marketing team hired another agency I worked with to pull together detailed profiles of the chief information officers (CIOs) of those 200 companies. The idea was that Scott would embark on a long-term effort to build relationships with the CIOs through personal outreach and phone calls, peer-to-peer introductions and high-end networking events that combined business meetings and elite pastimes, like golf. At the time, McNealy owned a home on the famed Pebble Beach golf course, and his team thought the prestigious venue would be a great hook to attract corporate CIOs.

But getting 200 of America's top CIOs to travel to California to attend a golf event was going to be a heavy lift. Even though McNealy was a major player in Silicon Valley, that didn't mean much to CIOs of companies like Ford, Procter & Gamble or Prudential. McNealy was humble enough to know this. Somehow, he had to make himself—and Sun—relevant to each invitee.

Though a junket to Pebble Beach to watch one of the world's most prestigious golf tournaments might sound like a must-attend boondoggle to the rest of us, Sun was playing in rarefied territory, and the odds of success were low. Top execs are invited to dozens—maybe even hundreds—of prestigious, high-end events every year. They pick and choose carefully, declining many invitations while passing others down to an SVP or VP to represent them—someone a little lower on the totem pole who would be happy to go to an all-expense-paid, luxury event.

The problem is that these less-senior folks aren't the key decision makers, and their presence dilutes the quality of the audience. The event then deteriorates into a room full of what some in the industry call "muffin eaters"—executives showing up for the appeal of the event who are not the power players that people like McNealy need to meet. And it gets worse: when the C-level attendees who do show up find themselves mingling with lower-level execs instead of their peers, they think, "Well, this is a disappointment" and bow out of future events. This audience-dilution spiral is deadly for event marketers, which is why planning C-level events is so terrifying. The negative cycle continues when management sees the cost-per-head of an event that failed to attract the right people: funding for the program gets cut, which makes attracting C-level people even harder.

Tech marketers were hungry to break this cycle of failure and poor return on investment, and I was determined to come up with a formula for success and become the go-to expert in this emerging niche. I began investigating C-level events, programs and engagement strategies to determine what worked and what didn't. I spoke to dozens of marketers, executives and agency leaders, identifying and analyzing the most successful C-level events and noting what they had in common.

What I learned was pretty simple: C-level people attend events that deliver two things: great thought-leadership content and peer-to-peer networking. While it was easier said than done, I had an idea on how to help companies succeed on both of these fronts.

With Sun Microsystems's CIO profiles, I was initially puzzled by the assignment. *This is going to be a piece of cake!* I thought. Google searches would easily surface the CIO bios, and I could just cut and paste them into a Word document! I was almost embarrassed—were they really going to pay me to do this busywork? But after a conversation with McNealy's team, I realized the assignment wasn't so simple. What they wanted was an in-depth dossier: insider information that couldn't be easily found through a search engine—discrete information about each individual that would make Sun stand out from its peers.

I worked with McNealy's team to create a basic template, filling it in as best I could for each executive. In addition to biographical information—like where they'd gone to school, where they'd worked—McNealy also wanted detail on their personal interests, current business initiatives, any notable quotes they'd delivered to the press or in a speech and any connections to other executives McNealy might know.

Suddenly, my simple cut-and-paste job looked pretty daunting. I refined the template and built out a few samples of real CIOs. It was hard work, especially the relationship mapping. I might find that McNealy served on a corporate board with a CIO's boss, for example, or I would uncover that Sun's own CIO sat on an industry council with another one of McNealy's target CIOs. I looked for any actionable path between McNealy and all 200 CIOs, so that even if Scott didn't know them directly, he had avenues to introduction through an intermediary. It was painstaking.

I discovered that McNealy was close with Jack Welch—the longtime, legendary CEO of General Electric—and that he was into hockey and golf. So I looked for anyone connected to Welch and also highlighted if they were fans of McNealy's favorite sports. If they were a golfer, I looked up their handicap, tournaments they'd attended and which celebrity golfers they had played with. The research was time-consuming, but it paid off. McNealy and his team were happy with the results.

I discovered it was equally important to learn what these CIOs *didn't* like. For example, one of the targets said explicitly in an interview that he had no interest in being the kind of elitist leader who schmoozed with colleagues on the golf course! I flagged this for McNealy's team, realizing an invitation to Pebble Beach would not only be a turn off, it would reveal that Sun hadn't taken the time to do its homework. I came across another interview in which a CIO emphatically stated she couldn't stand executives who spouted industry jargon. I flagged this as well: if Scott should catch her on the phone, he should dial the jargon way back.

As I honed my investigatory skills, I learned the value of digging deep: I could provide insight on what these executives cared about—thereby carving a path for my clients to win an introduction—as well as alert them on topics to avoid, to prevent them from damaging a budding relationship.

Sun improved the audience quality at its C-level events and kept the muffin eaters at bay, and it wasn't long before I was applying this new methodology across the board for my consulting clients. Or trying to, anyway...I had to convince clients that they needed to flip their event-planning process.

The current strategy was failing: designing an event tailored to the hosting company's own goals, promoting it to the desired invitees and reacting to RSVPs as they came in. If the right people weren't committing, they might expand the invite list or (heaven forbid) allow the muffin eaters to flood in, compromising the quality of the audience and the event. I'd seen so many C-level events end in an unfortunate scramble to get butts in seats—an act of self-sabotage I knew I could turn around.

One day, I asked a client, "What if you kicked off event planning with your ideal guest list, then designed an event around what *they* care about? And what if you sent each of them a highly personalized invitation from one of your top executives, calling out something that's relevant to them right now? Don't you think they'd be more likely to attend?"

I knew my research could answer the most important question for event marketers: how do we attract the people we most want? My clients were intrigued, but most thought it would be too difficult to execute. Undeterred, I proposed the process to companies all over the Valley, and a few agreed to pilot this methodology on a small scale. Others called me at the eleventh hour, desperate to salvage events that were just a month away because their C-level RSVP lists were not looking good. I was always eager to help—it gave me one more opportunity to test and prove what I believed to be true: creating hyper-personalized events for a C-level audience was well worth the effort and investment, and would close bigger deals, faster.

Convinced that executive research was crucial to both event design and audience acquisition strategy, I also recognized that it took too long to do everything bespoke. The timelines were too short, and it was expensive. Then it dawned on me: every tech company in Silicon Valley was chasing the same 2,500 or so executives...so it was conceivable that I could build and maintain a small database of C-level executives to provide all this information on demand. I could carve a niche, compiling in-depth dossiers on C-suite execs to separate my clients from their competitors.

In 2008, I copyrighted the template I'd been using and hatched a plan to build an executive profile database. And I registered a domain name for the product: Boardroom Insiders.

CHAPTER SEVEN
Full-Time Side Hustle

AS THE YEARS PASSED, the tech clients who hired me through Paolo would move to other companies and hire us again, so I had more business than I could handle—making more money than I ever had in my life, but I knew my fee was a fraction of what the agencies were charging their end clients.

My agency relationships proved to be invaluable, and one woman in particular became a critical mentor and supporter. Mary had toiled in the trenches in big tech for years. She viewed executive engagement and account-based marketing as essential and was a strong believer in the work I was doing, connecting me to people who were interested in doing experiments and pilot projects. One business unit she supported did business with only 30 corporations in the whole world—why shouldn't they have relationships with every C-level executive at those companies?

I was beginning to have similar conversations with other consulting clients. Encouraged, I told my agency partners that I was launching BI and that from then on, I would consult exclusively in the area of C-level marketing. If I was going to make a go of building a company, I needed to focus only on projects that would advance my goal.

Boardroom Insiders started out as a tool for my consulting work, and it remained that way for a few years. I had only a couple hundred executive profiles at first—mainly from the 30 or so enterprise accounts I knew the tech giants were most interested in. I made sure to have these targeted profiles locked and loaded so I could easily pull them when I was pitching clients. And every time I completed a request for new profiles, I added them to my database. It was hard to stay ahead of the demand: in addition to doing new research, I had to keep the existing profiles current, so I was constantly scrambling in the background to keep the BI database up to date. The beauty of it was that I was getting paid to build bespoke dossiers—and I owned all the content, which I could then repurpose for other clients and use to expand my database.

When the database reached critical mass, I'd make it available for a subscription fee. But what was critical mass, exactly? I wasn't sure, even as it reached 400, 500, 600 profiles. I had the beginnings of a self-service tool, but all my clients wanted me to package, customize and spoon-feed everything to them. I couldn't break free of consulting—and it was also paying the bills.

The Boardroom Insiders 1.0 website was not impressive. The user interface was clunky, and it wasn't even a real database: what I had was just a library of profiles, formatted as flat PDFs. When I built the website, I had a vision of random businesspeople finding it on the internet and plunking down their credit card to buy my profiles. The money would just come rolling in! What today sounds naive was actually possible then. Back in 2008, the internet wasn't very "crowded" yet, so getting visibility and acquiring customers was not nearly as difficult as it is today.

But the site garnered few visitors and remained primarily a tool for my C-level consulting work and a repository for PDF profiles I had to keep updating. I realized I could outsource the profile maintenance, but when BI 1.0 fell flat, I was at an impasse. I was a 43-year-old exhausted working mom seeking a four-hour work week. Heck, I would've been happy with a four-hour workday! I didn't know if I should continue to invest in Boardroom Insiders, and I was ready to call it quits...but I kept going anyway.

And then BI got its first paying customer: a marketing executive at Lockheed Martin who contacted me out of the blue after landing on the website. She was under the gun and needed a bunch of information on some executives very quickly—literally, the next day—because Lockheed was prepping for a big meeting, and she had neither the time nor the know-how to pull the information together herself. I didn't have the profiles on the executives she wanted, but I didn't tell *her* that. I asked if we could deliver the profiles the next morning.

"I'd like to give one of our analysts an opportunity to refresh these for you and make sure they're completely up to date," I fibbed.

Then Andrew and I stayed up nearly all night composing the profiles. She was thrilled to get them so quickly and was amazed at the quality.

"Can I give you my first born?" she exclaimed.

BI's second customer worked for the state of Virginia's economic development office, gathering information on companies and their leaders, with the goal of convincing them to set up regional offices or move their headquarters to Virginia. Her use case was something I didn't even know existed. In those early days, I was still trying to learn who needed my profiles and why—but I told people I had the info at the ready, while in reality, I was scrambling in the background, assembling the profiles on the fly—some, literally overnight. When the news broke about Elizabeth Holmes and Theranos, the parallels were not lost on me. Like me, she had a Potemkin product, requiring a mad scramble behind the scenes to create the illusion that it magically worked.

When Meredith from Virginia signed up for a $300 yearly subscription to the database, it had just 250 profiles. So I agreed she could request new profiles on anyone else she wanted. Meredith was the first customer to commit to an annual subscription, and she stayed with us for years. Every time I read about a big company relocating to Virginia I thought of her, hoping we had played a small part in the deal.

BI's third paying customer was a real head-scratcher, but who was I to argue with someone who wanted to get on board? An executive from ConAgra's Lamb Weston division also found us through the website. His division sold massive amounts of potato-based appetizers to restaurant chains: potato skins, potato croquettes, tater tots, etc. I asked him why on earth one would need to discuss frozen potatoes in the C-suite, and he explained that they wanted to start conversations with restaurant chain CFOs (like TGI Fridays, Applebee's) about how the margins on frozen potato appetizers are incredibly high. He wanted to spread the word about ConAgra's innovative line of sophisticated potato flavor profiles. Potato skins are supposed to be cheap, but a restaurant could charge more for a dish like "potato bacon croquettes" because it sounds fancy—but it's still made from the same inexpensive ingredients. In food service parlance, he needed to pitch CFOs on how ConAgra could help them drive menu innovation while reaping huge margins.

I was blown away that BI's first database subscribers came from such unexpected places. All of them had problems they needed to solve and were willing to overlook the small and limited scale of the tool if we could provide even a partial, imperfect solution. It was these little wins—and the future they foreshadowed—that kept me going.

With BI gaining traction, I needed to start farming out work —not just the profile maintenance, but the fresh research as well. When I was consulting for Scott McNealy at Sun, I'd hired a few contractors to help me with the research. I had to pay a premium for the right talent—a high degree of business acumen was required, and they had to be tenacious and creative researchers of the no-stone-unturned variety. This resulted in an eye-popping price point that would be unsustainable. I was never going to be able to scale the database to critical mass.

I'd been pondering this problem for a couple of months when a man named George Plosker reached me by phone after coming upon the Boardroom Insiders website.

"I think it's really cool what you're doing," he said. "But it must be really expensive. Have you ever thought of offshoring the research?"

George was a salesperson for an offshore research and data collection firm in India. I told him I'd considered it, but I didn't think it would work because the profiles required not only excellent English-language skills but also an understanding of American companies, executive roles and business jargon. I was skeptical.

"Well, given your cost structure, what's the percentage that would be worth it for you? If they got you 60 or 70 percent of the way there, would that make it worthwhile?"

I understood what he was saying: if they got me 70 percent of the way to a bespoke profile, the profiles would just need editing as opposed to someone compiling them from scratch—a big timesaver. That could cut my costs dramatically while maintaining the quality.

He suggested we do a test run. I agreed to give it a try.

I'm terrible at remembering names and even whole events, but I've never forgotten George—I was so impressed with how he approached me so thoughtfully and earnestly. He identified my pain points, anticipated my concerns and proposed a solution. He also changed my mind by showing me it wasn't an all-or-nothing situation, and even an imperfect, partial solution could transform my costs. His cold call led to a 14-year relationship with an India-based firm that ran our dedicated Boardroom Insiders research team under the guidance of George's then-colleague, Matt Manning.

Though we had significant training to do to get the work where we needed it to be, the research team in India was ramping up nicely. Matt's dad had worked in academia in India, and he'd grown up there and understood the culture and how to get things done. I could see a path to success as his team took on more of the profile research work, but as Matt and I mapped out the workflow, we saw another problem: the database was a collection of flat PDF files that needed constant updating. It would make no sense for his team to work in those files if we were going to convert them into a database at a later time.

I couldn't bring Matt's content management team fully onboard until the database was built, and that would cost me big bucks I didn't have. But Matt knew some Indian software engineers with full-time jobs who could moonlight to build the BI database—for a fraction of the cost of a US-based company.

The proposal was intriguing, but I'd still have to come up with the money—and I was overwhelmed by the idea of getting outside capital. As an introvert, I wasn't a great networker, and my experience with Fidget made me wary of investors. But this time, luck and timing were on my side.

While my networking skills were lacking, Andrew was the complete opposite. He is a genuine people person who maintains strong relationships with almost everyone he's ever met. One of his friends was a serial entrepreneur named Michael Blend, who had recently hit it big with a company called HotKeys. Using internet domain registration data, HotKeys contacted people who owned loads of domain names and weren't doing anything with them.

En-masse domain registration speculation was a thing back in those days. People would buy up a bunch of domains in hopes of selling or otherwise monetizing them later. For example, one person bought up all the domains for different dog breeds: Bostonterrier.com, labradorretriever.com and so on. Hotkeys approached these domain owners and offered a simple monetization scheme for the dormant sites. They would add graphics and cute dog photos at the top of the page, along with some simple copy, then load the rest of the page with Google AdWords listings related to the topic: ads for pet toy sites, veterinarians and so on. Clicks drove ad revenue, and HotKeys split it with the domain owners. It was a no-brainer for the site owners: they didn't have to do anything but collect the money.

Michael had hired Andrew to generate graphics and copy for the sites. It sounded like a scam to me, but when I saw it was completely legit and throwing off tons of cash with very low effort, I was impressed. Initially, Michael offered Andrew equity in HotKeys in lieu of pay, but after surviving the first dot-com bust where everyone with equity ended up with nothing, I was leery about taking the risk. We needed cash to pay our bills. On my insistence, Andrew told Michael he'd prefer pay over equity. It was not a good decision. When Michael sold the company, Andrew would have made a few million if he'd taken the equity. Michael was gracious enough to give Andrew a nice bonus for his participation in making HotKeys successful, but I felt like a chump—that payoff would have eliminated the financial pressure we were feeling as a young family living in one of the most expensive cities in the world.

Michael was an unassuming, fun guy—an affable goofball with a great laugh. When I first got to know him, I had no inkling he was a mogul in the making. His success with HotKeys was no isolated stroke of good luck; a classic serial entrepreneur, he's been involved in quite a few successful startups and exits. Today, he's the CEO of a publicly traded company.

Andrew encouraged me to get Michael's advice when I was

trying to launch BI, but I found his success intimidating. I was afraid he would see that I didn't know what I was doing, or that I hadn't made much progress even though I'd validated the need for my product with the biggest tech companies on the planet.

I finally got up the nerve to talk to Michael about what I was trying to do. What interested him most was the premium nature of Boardroom Insiders, as evidenced by the fact that Scott McNealy's team had paid $1,000 for each executive profile.

"If you put that in a database—even if you're charging $200 per profile—that's a lot of money! Seriously, Sharon, you should quit consulting and focus on this. It could be really big." He looked me dead in the eye.

Whoa.

"Well," I waffled, "I've done enough market validation to believe this could be a successful business, but…I don't have the money to build out the database."

"I'll give you the money to build it. I'll write you a check right now."

Shit.

I knew that if I took Michael's money, I'd have to conquer my fears and self-doubt—deliver a functional product and build a sustainable business.

"You're kidding. What would you be willing to invest?"

"How about $125k…for 10 percent of the company? We'll start there. I can put in more if needed, as long as I stay at 10 percent."

My heart was thumping in my chest. Was I going to commit to this? Believe in myself and make this happen?

I took his offer.

I was scared. Michael was a personal friend, and I had to make this work. I was determined not to lose his money.

So after my meeting with Michael, I had the cash to build the website from the little shell it was into a proper, self-service database product. I focused on building out the relationship-mapping component, a data niche that was pretty sophisticated at the time. I told Matt Manning to get his content team lined up and ready to work. And we were off. Michael's investment propelled me forward, and there was no turning back now.

In the beginning, the editorial work—although better than expected—still required heavy editing. But once I got into the rhythm of providing painstakingly detailed feedback, the work coming out of the team in India steadily improved. As the years rolled by and BI grew—and the volume of information on the internet exploded—the team's research actually became *too* comprehensive. In the early days, I'd instructed them to add every bit of information into the profiles they could find. But the dossiers were becoming too bloated, and privacy concerns rose to the forefront: we didn't want to include things like DUIs or the value of a person's home. Over time, I guided them not only on what to include, but what to avoid. The team was responsive to any direction I provided, and as we got into a good working rhythm, I came to rely on them more and more.

Michael's investment also allowed me to hire a team to develop the website. And once it was up and running, I had a functioning database, roughly five hundred profiles and a team in India doing a good job of maintaining them. I had little ongoing business to support it, but the enthusiasm and encouragement from my consulting clients inspired me to keep going. Whenever I walked into meetings and showed them what I had, everyone leaned forward. And they always wanted more.

I'd ask them one question: "Imagine you had this kind of information on *all* of your target executives—what could you do with it?"

As I sat back and watched my customers consider the impact of the tool I was offering them, I realized I was finally throwing off the shackles of my upbringing and seeing everything in a new light—the potential was immense, and I was ready to embrace it. As a child, I was taught to not dream too big—to never get my hopes up so I wouldn't be disappointed. "Nothing will probably come of it," I used to tell myself. How could I possibly succeed when I was constantly telling myself that I probably wouldn't? It was difficult to break away from that thought pattern, but with the creation of Boardroom Insiders, I really had no other choice.

As BI developed, I dabbled with the idea of raising some money and met with a few venture capital firms. They really hammered me on the scalability of my human-centered research process. I always countered that my customers loved our profiles and that the quality of our content was unmatched. That was the whole point. I was sitting in a San Francisco coffee shop when one VC interrupted my pitch: "Stop talking about the quality of your content. No one cares!"

I was so earnest; I replied, "Well, my customers care. Isn't that what really matters?"

The VCs were not the only naysayers.

When you're just getting started, every meeting seems like a make-or-break situation. As an entrepreneur, I had to develop resilience so that one bad meeting didn't send me into a death spiral. When I pitched the idea of C-suite engagement to a senior marketer from Xerox, he was witheringly dismissive: "I just don't buy it. I don't care about reaching the C-suite. And even if I did, who gives a shit if someone likes golf? No one's going to make a multimillion-dollar decision based on whether they play golf or not."

Fortunately, I'd seen how wrong he was, and I was able to dismiss this marketer as a clueless dud. Putting aside his ignorance of the fact that doing business on the golf course was most definitely a thing, what he couldn't grasp was that it's not just about someone liking golf—it's about caring enough to learn about the people you want to do business with so you can build authentic, trusted relationships based on common interests. It was obvious to me, but not everyone could wrap their heads around the concept, and many weren't willing to put in the effort. But there were solid wins that kept me going.

At Boardroom Insiders we developed our own template based on what our customers wanted to know. Our analysts mined the information from a variety of sources, cut and pasted it into our template and sourced it to our clients. We never plagiarized: we said exactly where we got it. We made the process more efficient over time, refining our training and processes, leveraging digital tools and developing our own software.

One day, a Fortune 50 tech company marketer called me in a panic. They were hosting a C-level event focused on "Models of Innovation." Despite having invested six figures in celebrity keynote speakers, they weren't getting the RSVPs they needed. I dug into what they meant by "Models of Innovation" and learned how challenging it is for large companies to innovate. Those that do it successfully do it in different ways: some set up innovation centers in partnership with universities, others form internal innovation teams to work on "blue sky" projects, while others have internal venture funds that invest in and monitor startups they might acquire.

The event had a compelling focus, but the client hadn't made it relevant to its intended audience. To them, it was just another boondoggle on a long list of invites. The strategy had been to send a generic email blast. I advised them they needed to resend personalized invites directly from the CEO or CTO and follow up with a round of phone calls from the executive's office. Reviewing their list of invitees, I gave them simple bullet points that would attract the interest of each executive. It was a ridiculous gambit, given how late it was, and I had to scramble to find information on each prospective attendee...but what I found was pure gold.

For example, the client had targeted the CIO of Progressive Insurance, and my research found that he was one of the pioneers of the now-ubiquitous, usage-based pricing for car insurance. My bullet point for him was: "You pioneered one of the biggest innovations in your industry in decades. We would love to have you come to our event and share with your peers how you were able to accomplish that within a large enterprise."

Around the same time, I attended a few industry conferences to explore the ecosystem of the business information space in which Boardroom Insiders (aka "BI") was carving its niche and had the chance to discuss BI with lawyers, accountants, venture capitalists, competitors and vendors like Matt Manning, whose company, IEI, was now enjoying rapid growth. I was even invited to speak and present BI a couple of times. The scalability challenges came up every time; it seemed to be all anyone cared about—if you couldn't get absolutely huge, why bother?

People had been in that industry so long that they couldn't see what was missing or imagine doing things differently. They were complacent about poor data quality and didn't find the needs and gaps I outlined compelling, even though I'd validated them with some of the largest companies in the world with the biggest marketing budgets. The industry comprised mainly older men who'd known each other forever and tended to elevate the latest wunderkinds who had raised a bunch of VC money. So while I felt like an interloper, I made a point of spending time with these guys at the conferences, listening and getting to know them. I did feel safe among them—which, as one of the few women there, was important.

The feedback I was receiving on Boardroom Insiders reprised my old feelings of imposter syndrome. One memory stands out as a metaphor for how I felt as I attempted to establish my industry bona fides. I was speaking on a panel, presenting Boardroom Insiders for the very first time. I put a lot of thought into my outfit, because when I look my best, I feel more confident. I was excited to wear these amazing, silver power pumps I loved but hadn't worn in a while. When I headed to the stage, the shoes felt loose and were slipping off my heels as I walked. *What the hell? Have my feet shrunk?* I struggled to keep it together and walk normally, curling my toes to prevent myself from stepping right out of my shoes. It's unlikely anyone noticed, but I was uncomfortable and embarrassed. I was in a room full of insiders and experts, trying to establish credibility with a product that violated all kinds of industry conventions—but I felt like a little kid playing dress-up, not able to fill the shoes I was trying to step into.

Not being truly accepted in this new industry could have quashed my determination. I don't know where I got the courage to keep going, but I was getting used to being the contrarian in the room, and I began to embrace it. I was an outsider who saw the industry as a complacent echo chamber. But I also understood exactly what my customers—some of the biggest tech companies in the world—wanted and saw a clear gap in the market I could fill. With few resources, I looked to VCs and the sector's biggest players for support and repeatedly came up short. I'm not a very confident person, but somehow I was able to shut out all the negative chatter and focus on my customers, who kept telling me that I had something special and that they wanted more.

As disappointing as it was to get dismissed so often by insiders, I never lost my conviction about BI. It didn't conform to the popular models, but that didn't mean it wasn't worthy. If I wasn't going to be the VC or industry darling of the moment, I had to find a different way in. Why couldn't these guys see that the ecosystem of the business information space was in danger of extinction if we continued on the same path? If they couldn't envision their way out of the mess they'd created, it might just take an outlier—a woman with the conviction to transform the ecosystem—to force a change.

But there was one big problem I needed to solve. I'm not great at networking, cold calling or small talk. Even with a warm introduction, I feel awkward. What can I say? I'm an introvert. If BI was going to gain real traction, I needed to orchestrate a major networking push and get my idea in front of a whole lot of people, fast. I wasn't exactly sure what I wanted or needed—I wasn't looking for funding, and I wasn't looking for partners. But I knew I needed a lot more contacts to help me get BI to the next level.

So I decided that for the entire month of August 2009, I would make at least one call every day to someone I thought could help me move my idea forward. It was a productive month. I enjoyed the conversations I had, and they left me feeling energized and inspired. I achieved my goal of one or more calls per day, and I connected with a handful of people who changed the game for my company. It turned out to be one of the most important things I ever did for the business.

My best networking contact was one of my first: Matt Manning, who turned out to be the Kevin Bacon of the information industry. He knows everybody and at some point has spoken or worked with most of the business information companies, from innovative startups to big legacy enterprises. Matt introduced me to Patrick Spain, the founder of Hoover's, my go-to resource when I worked in localization sales. Hoover's started out as a printed book for sales, marketing and business development teams looking for contact information on prospective customers. Talking to Patrick was the industry equivalent of talking to a rock star. He'd created a fantastic product and went on to sell Hoover's to Dun & Bradstreet, a huge achievement. Like a lot of people in the industry, Patrick challenged me on the scale issue, but having maintained a large editorial team himself for Hoover's (which is why their content shined), he understood why human labor was an important element of my model.

Patrick then introduced me to Bobby Martin, who had sold his own industry research tool, called First Research, to

Hoover's/ Dun & Bradstreet. Bobby was hugely supportive and also empathetic. Having experienced the same challenges and pain I was feeling, his content was also curated by humans, so he'd also been the uncool kid on the block when it came to the VCs. Bobby didn't sugarcoat how hard it was to break through to success.

"Sharon, I used to cry real tears," he exclaimed. "I used to wake up and say every morning: 'How do I get somebody to buy this stuff?'"

His struggle and his ultimate success inspired me and kept me going. Bobby echoed Michael Blend's sentiment that I needed to devote myself completely to BI. He didn't like the fact that I was doing full-time consulting while I was trying to get the company off the ground.

"I don't care what you do," he said, "take out a second mortgage if you have to, but focus 100 percent on BI. It's the only way it's going to work."

I didn't know how in the hell I could quit my consulting work. I was the primary (and often only) breadwinner in my family of four.

CHAPTER EIGHT

The Swashbuckler and the Salesman

BOBBY CALLED me every now and then to check in. One day, he said, "I have this buddy—we went to college together and he worked for me at First Research. He's great. He had a three-year earn-out at Dun & Bradstreet after they bought us, and he's going to be wrapping that up soon. You should talk to him. He's looking for something new."

And that's how I came to meet Lee.

Bobby and Lee met in college, then worked together at Bank of America. When Bobby left and started First Research—an industry information company that crafted in-depth industry profiles for commercial bankers—Lee joined him. Bobby developed the product, and Lee and another one of their buddies, Wil Brawley, were his salesmen. The industry profiles First Research compiled were similar to Boardroom Insiders' executive dossiers, but they were tailored to commercial banks selling into manufacturing, healthcare and many other industries. Their clients ate up the information—so much so that First Research was a runaway success, and when it sold to Dun & Bradstreet, they made money. They had a lot of fun, too.

While Lee had the right background, I wasn't really looking for a partner. But I knew I needed a sales whiz if BI was going to move to the next level—someone who had worked in the business information industry and could get BI in front of the right people. Surely those responsible for executive programs like global account-based marketing and heads of strategic accounts would see the value we were offering. Up to that point, my sales efforts had been limited to my consulting customers, and C-suite sales was still in its nascent state. Anyone fronting the sales push for BI would have a huge challenge to tackle.

Lee maintained that top salespeople require industry intelligence, company intelligence and executive intelligence. He saw it as a pyramid. At the base are the issues facing the industry that can impact a deal—for example, manufacturing might be negatively impacted by a weather disaster or other supply chain disruption. The next level of the pyramid is company intelligence. How are industry-wide issues affecting a specific company, and what's the strategy for responding? Companies react to industry issues in different ways, with varying degrees of success, so presuming every company is in the same boat is a false assumption that could trip up a salesperson. At the top of the pyramid is executive intelligence, which was BI's focus. A salesperson pitching a chief information officer on outsourcing some of its IT services would want to know if that CIO had led an insourcing or outsourcing effort for their past employer. I was an expert in the top layer of the pyramid, and at First Research, Lee had developed expertise selling the base layer.

I knew Lee could be a great salesperson for BI, but Bobby pitched him hard as a full-on partner. I hadn't considered that, but the more I engaged with Lee, the more I saw how our personalities and skills complemented each other. I'm impulsive —I follow my gut instincts and am quick to say, "Let's go for it." Lee was more conservative: "Wait a minute, let's take a step back and make sure we have all our ducks in a row." He also had the skill set to build a sales team.

We began talking on the phone in September of 2009, and I

flew out to North Carolina to meet him the following month. I was pretty sold on Lee after our first in-person meeting. I could see he was a really good fit: in addition to his sales and industry experience, he had a strong finance background, which I lacked. But—true to his deliberate, cautious nature—Lee wasn't ready to commit.

Over the course of about nine months, we got to know one another. And the more I got to know him, the more I agreed with Bobby that I'd be fortunate to have him as my partner. While our skill sets were very different, they complemented one another, and we shared the same values. Lee was trustworthy, authentic and smart. I was excited about having him join me. I'd call or email when I had a win—like completing a milestone or capturing the interest of a new prospect.

"Hey, Lee. Hope the family's well?"

"All good here. You?"

"Terrific. In fact, I was calling to let you know we just landed another big project. Gonna need some extra hands on deck. I'd like to continue the conversation about bringing you fully onboard."

"Who's the client?"

"It's another project for Cisco."

"Great news. What do they need? What's the commitment?"

"We're still figuring that out, but…they're huge, the project is huge. This will bring in a lot of revenue."

"How do you know that if you don't know what you're delivering yet?"

"Lee, they're *huge.*"

"Such a *swashbuckler*…"

"What?"

"You're a swashbuckler, Sharon. Plowing into the waves without checking the weather or the marine chart first."

"OK, Lee…whatever you say."

In truth, offering up a chunk of my company was a big decision, but the more I dealt with Lee, the more I was convinced he would be a critical linchpin to Boardroom Insiders' success. When Lee officially joined BI in July of 2010, our little ship gained a rudder. He knew more than I about certain aspects of the business that were critical to our success, and his skills were completely additive. Boardroom Insiders was poised to launch.

Both Michael Blend and Bobby Martin were pushing me to devote 100 percent of my time and efforts to BI. And taking Michael's money meant I had an obligation—I had to make BI happen. This created huge pressure for me. I told Michael how excited I was about Lee joining me, and how perfect he was to catapult BI to success. The three of us had a call, and Michael instinctively leaned into Lee's skill set. The two of them could talk more easily about sales—they spoke the same language around finance and deals. Lee explained his vision for building a sales infrastructure and his strategy for structuring deals. Michael was excited. He saw BI as the little engine that could.

Lee also brought an incredible network of people with him. He lives in a suburb of Charlotte, where everyone's very social and many work in tech-adjacent businesses—making them low-hanging fruit for us, sales-wise. The joke was that no matter what we needed, Lee always knew "a guy in his neighborhood" who was a good lead. Whether we were looking for an accountant, a web developer or an M&A banker, we found experts through his neighborhood network—our first successful sales guy was the brother of someone Lee knew socially, and a lot of our key hires were people he met through his contacts in the Charlotte area.

There were a couple of areas where Lee and I were similar. As glass-half-empty types, we saw all the gaps and flaws in our business model, and we worried about the clunkiness of our early product. As time went on and we both had more skin in the game, we tended to be fear-driven. Since we both had young kids, there was a lot to be afraid of, and we weren't even paying ourselves in those early days of our partnership.

But there were areas where we differed. Lee worried we weren't airtight on our deals—leaving ourselves open contractually so that customers could easily cancel orders or fight us if things went sideways. He'd had more exposure to the business end of things, whereas I was the scrappy consultant, used to swashbuckling around with nothing on paper to protect me— delivering on projects without so much as a purchase order. Lee was also nervous about "budget dumping"—where a customer who was about to see a chunk of its department budget expire would ask us to invoice them for a large amount before we even had time to negotiate the deliverables.

I was also in the habit of agreeing to big custom projects that had little to do with our database product. I argued that, in a time when we were both working without pay and had barely enough to stay afloat, we couldn't afford to turn away anyone's money. Lee agreed, on one condition: our long game had to focus on building our database subscription business—our only path to the holy grail of annual recurring revenue (ARR). Our shared goal was to sell the company someday, and we knew the sale price wouldn't take into account any custom project revenue but would be driven 100 percent by our ARR number. I was relieved to have Lee as a partner who would shepherd us cautiously and bring in industry experience, new ideas and discipline.

Lee and I spent our first year together picking apart our product. Working from his one-man office in Fort Mill, South Carolina, he reached out to his network and former customers to get their thoughts about BI. We created a list of experiments, like doing a Google ad run, buying up the names of keywords of people in our database. It failed miserably when people searching for "Michael Jackson" clicked on the link for a CEO with the same name and exhausted our daily ad budget by 8 am one day. We ran many such experiments over the years, and we were moving too fast to beat ourselves up or cry about the money we wasted if something failed.

"We've been wanting to try that for a long time…and now we know it doesn't work!" I'd say.

"Mm-hmm." I could hear Lee grimacing on the other end of the phone.

We were wearing so many hats and had so much to think about, it was a relief to be able to check something off our list—even if it was a failure—and move on to the next thing. Learning and quickly moving on from failure became core to our culture as we grew our team.

One of our more successful marketing experiments involved compiling a list of all of the Fortune 500 chief information officers and posting it on the BI website to download for free. This offering remained our most popular piece of content bait for years. Our existing customers loved it, and it was a good source of leads for new customers. We included statistics with the list: the percentage of CIOs who were women, immigrants and so on. *The Wall Street Journal* picked it up pretty regularly, crediting BI as the source, so I personally put a great deal of effort into making sure the information was 100 percent accurate—which required painstaking research underlying the principle of "defensibility" I was carrying forward from my days at *San Diego Magazine.*

I was jolted awake from my dream of defensibility one day when I discovered one of the CIOs we were profiling had been dead for some time. The "dead exec" story served as a model cautionary tale, and defensibility became part of our culture, serving us well for years to come. Everyone on our team came to understand that the best way to insulate ourselves from criticism was to ensure a clear rationale and that thorough research supported every decision. If and when a customer questioned our data or why we did something a certain way, we had a logical, defensible answer.

As we built BI together, it began to feel like a family business —and sometimes it literally was. I occasionally hired my teenagers to do data entry, and during crunch times, both our spouses pitched in to get projects done. Our employees and their kids even pitched in to assemble furniture when we moved offices. We would have put Lee's kids to work too, but they were too young!

Michael Blend offered advice that was often instrumental in growing Boardroom Insiders—but he was used to playing in much larger, better-resourced pools—and most of his advice required thinking way bigger than Lee and I imagined we could afford. Michael would frequently call us from a dirt road in Hawaii on his way to a secret surfing spot.

"Sharon. Lee. Listen, I had an idea on the—" Static.

The connection was spotty, and we'd catch only half of what he was saying on his way to catch his next wave.

"What's that, Michael? You're breaking up."

"Okay. Hang on. So here's what you do—" Static.

He talked really fast and had a way of making things sound easy—when for us, they weren't.

On one call, he told us, "Just hire 20 more salespeople! You'll probably have to fire half of them—but in the end, some will work out."

Lee and I looked at each other—*20* salespeople?

"Michael, we're struggling to pay the rent here. Even if we had the cash, we still don't have a repeatable sales model, so…"

"Lee, you've got to ride with me on this one. It'll work!"

And then there was the competition. While we didn't yet have any, that didn't stop us from worrying. For years, Lee and I lived in fear that a well-funded competitor would come along and eat our lunch. But after a while, that appeared to be less and less likely.

Why? Because no one wanted to do what we were doing! It was just too hard and didn't have the potential in terms of exit value: it was a lot of effort, involved too many humans, was too hard to scale and —because of a few big, bad actors—companies that traded in data about people were under more regulatory scrutiny than ever before. Who would be crazy enough to build such a business?

So we didn't have to worry about direct competitors or commoditization—but that didn't mean we didn't have to compete for budget dollars. Our closest budget competitor was LinkedIn Sales Navigator—a veritable Goliath (owned by Microsoft) to our little David. We used LinkedIn all day as a source and a sales tool, but when it came to what our customers needed, there was no question our profiles were demonstrably more comprehensive. Our sales team regularly showed prospective customers a LinkedIn profile side by side against one of ours to demonstrate the added content and value.

We now had over a thousand profiles in our database, ready to go. Our India team had also developed a tracking tool, so that if one of the execs moved on to another job or company, we'd have the revised profile polished up and published within a day. Competition, check. Product, check. We were pretty well locked and loaded. Our remaining threat was that prospective customers would bail on C-suite research altogether, because it was too expensive and hard to scale.

But we knew our existing customers. While most companies still didn't have the resources for BI's in-depth dossiers, the top salespeople we served saw it as a must-have. Lee and I liked to imagine them sitting down with a beer or glass of wine on a Sunday night to prep for a big meeting in the coming week. They needed insight into the company and its people to feel confident going into their pitch. So they spent their own time reading annual reports, earnings transcripts, interviews and articles featuring top company executives. These were the exceptional salespeople, our bread and butter—the top performers with high business acumen who knew it paid off to meticulously map their talking points to company business initiatives and executive "care-abouts."

We were poised to spoon-feed our information directly to top-performing salespeople, freeing up their time. But as we thought about our pitch, it dawned on us that the biggest problem was being able to tell them what was in our database.

"I can't sell this if I can't tell people what's in it." Lee had stated the obvious.

We had around 1,200 profiles: mostly CIOs, most in the Fortune 500, but some in the public sector, some in Europe. Our database was all over the place.

"I can't sell this until we can draw a box around the data. We need to be able to tell prospective customers exactly what they'll be getting."

I blanched, embarrassed I'd never thought of this before.

So we got to work defining the minimally acceptable "box" of data we needed for Lee to confidently take the product to market. We called it the "Fortune 500 top five." For each Fortune 500 company, we would have profiles for the CEO, CFO, COO, CMO and CIO. We chose the roles and the companies based on what our prospects were asking for. And we'd need at least 2,500 profiles to have our box ready to sell.

Lee, Bobby Martin and Wil Brawley came up with some money, and Michael Blend put in a little more to maintain his 10 percent stake in the company. I hired more editorial free-lancers, and we all worked at a feverish pace. We had to build the box by the end of the summer.

The best part of having Lee as a partner was that we were doing a lot in less time now. While the company grossed a couple hundred thousand in revenue our first year together, most of it came from custom projects, not subscriptions. And after covering our costs, we still weren't making enough to pay ourselves what we needed to make. Building the box was the key to our survival. Our financial cushions were wearing thin, and we both had our share of sleepless nights.

By this time, we'd both put so much into BI, failure was not an option. I was not going to lose Michael's money. I was not going to let down Lee's family and mine. I'd put so much of myself into BI, I could not fail in middle age. Not now. No way in hell.

CHAPTER NINE
The Double Sell

OUR BOX of 2,500 profiles had officially launched, but Lee and I were still struggling on the sales side. I'd always resisted positioning BI as a data company because the data market is commoditized and swarming with competition. I saw BI as an insight and content company, with a strong editorial focus. The quality of our product was dependent upon humans—not computers: our team of highly trained analysts brought the value to the product. Once we'd earned a customer's business and they started using us, they got it. They could see the difference. But closing customers was a challenge because we were priced at a premium compared to the data scrapers.

Prospective customers were skeptical about our price point. They were also jaded—data vendors notoriously overpromised and underdelivered. We were the opposite, but it seemed too good to be true. If we didn't have what they needed, they could request it and get it within two days? They'd believe it when they saw it. We'd usually do better than that, delivering custom profiles within 24 hours. Customers were delighted: "*Wow!* This is amazing! Thank you so much for the quick turnaround!" We offered a lot of handholding too, making sure each customer had multiple points of contact if they needed help.

I was beginning to think my years of consulting for big tech had given me a false sense of what was going on in the market. It was a scary notion, since Lee and I had spent the past 18 months building a whole business around the premise of C-suite engagement. Listening to Lee's accounts of sales calls and sitting in on a few pitches myself, I began to realize we were way ahead of the market. While tech behemoths like Sun, Cisco and EMC were leveraging C-suite engagement to huge advantage, the rank-and-file tech world just wasn't there yet.

Lee would spend the first 10 minutes of sales meetings convincing prospects that C-suite selling was important—before he could even pitch Boardroom Insiders. He coined a term for the phenomenon: the "Double Sell." You know the stock photo of the guy trying to roll a boulder uphill? That was Lee—and by extension, me. A surprising number of prospects—while intrigued with what we were evangelizing—would conclude that the benefits were unproven at best, and we were relegated to a "nice-to-have."

We faced another challenge, even with people who found our profiles potentially game-changing for their company. They often had no idea how to act on the information. This is where Lee would bring me in. This was my wheelhouse—what I'd done during all those years of consulting. Give me a nugget of information about an executive, and I can give you at least three actionable ideas on how to use it. Say a customer was profiling attendees coming to their event: I'd pull out nuggets of data with recommendations on how to use the information to get the invitees to network with each other.

I called it "facilitated networking." For example, sit a group of CIOs who all began their careers at IBM at one table, and arrange the rest of the attendees according to commonalities as well. An MC could prompt them with an announcement: "Each of you has something in common with everyone at your table. You've got five minutes to figure out what it is." You could even have the tables compete to see which one discovers the common thread first.

Marketers loved these types of ideas, but they were fearful of trying something new with such a high-powered customer audience. I encouraged them by appealing to our common humanity: "Yes, they are powerful. Yes, they are important. But they're *people*, just like you and me. And most people don't like the initial awkwardness of networking events—those first few moments of breaking the ice are an uncomfortable struggle for everyone. Help smooth the way, and they will always remember the experience and also admire your creativity and boldness!"

But, given the risk aversion prevalent at these big organizations, my recommendations weren't executed as often as I'd like.

But month after month, our subscriber count steadily grew, and more importantly, existing customers were renewing their subscriptions. Our ability to retain customers gave us more confidence. We were also getting positive feedback. We'd hear: "I've been trying to get a meeting with this guy for a year—and I took one little snippet from your profile, referenced it in an email and he got back to me in five minutes!"

Some subscribers sent executives football jerseys of their favorite teams, or coffee-table books about collectible cars to car fanatics. Sending gifts based on personal info can be a little risky because it can feel creepy. I enjoy Zumba, but if someone I'd never met sent me a sales package with a Zumba shirt, I'd be a little alarmed! I'd advise customers that the best thing to do when just getting started is to reference a business initiative the executive is passionate about. C-level engagement pays off when you approach it like nurturing a garden with drip irrigation. You don't plant a seed, dump a whole bucket of water on it then walk away and leave it alone for months, expecting good results. A relationship, like a seedling, needs consistent nurturing over time...drip, drip, drip. The payoff doesn't happen right away, but when it does, it bears fruit for many years to come.

Bottom line, things were really tough those first two years of our partnership. Between 2010 and 2012, we still weren't paying ourselves, and it was hard to be strategic about targeting prospective customers because we just needed money coming in the door. So we took on clients we probably shouldn't have, which could suck our resources dry on specialized projects that weren't contributing to our primary goal of building our subscription business and our ARR. We'd let customers pay us $10,000 a year for custom profiles that didn't help us grow. One customer throwing a star-studded event bogged down our editorial team with requests for profiles on Barack Obama, Vladimir Putin and Martina Navratilova—profiles our core customers would never use—so they just gummed up the database.

We could also see when customers weren't using the database—some never logged in once. But we kept taking their money because we needed every penny. If we had any hope of selling the company one day, taking on bad-fit customers would depress our usage data and our renewal rates, jeopardizing our prospects for the highest multiple possible. Bad-fit customers also ate up our editorial team's valuable time. Customers like the frozen potato appetizer company weren't going to help us close a deal with Salesforce or VMware.

Then there was the budget dump. A windfall of cash in the coffers should be a good thing, business-wise, right? Not in this case. Marketers protect their budgets obsessively, doing whatever it takes to ensure they don't get cut. Toward the end of a fiscal quarter or just before year-end, we'd experience a frenzy of budget dumping—where marketing clients dumped their remaining budget for the quarter or the year to justify their budgets going forward.

BI benefited hugely from budget dumping, and I absolutely

loved it. One minute, we didn't know how we were going to pay ourselves, and suddenly $40,000 would drop from the sky. Lee didn't like it at all, because these were arbitrary, one-off deals instead of the recurring revenue we needed to build to fetch the highest possible sale price when it came time to sell the company. It made our revenue look unpredictable and lumpy. And if the client didn't have the budget to dump the next year, it would increase our churn—a red flag to buyers and investors.

But budget dumping helped BI survive, and I was enthusiastic about any money that came our way.

Lee would ask, "Is there a database subscription in there somewhere?"

This is why he was such a great partner—he was always focused on the recurring revenue that would ultimately determine BI's valuation and sale price. He insisted we stop taking on projects that didn't add to our recurring revenue. Like Bobby, he was concerned that these one-off consulting engagements took my focus away from the part of the business that really mattered. We had to focus on scalability, developing a set process and a pricing model that would grow our ARR—or we could say goodbye to our dream of selling the business one day.

We had to wrestle with other annoyances that come with having an online business. Credit card thieves started using our site to test the validity of stolen credit card numbers. They'd buy a single profile as a test and if the transaction went through, they knew the card was safe to use. We'd get calls from irate scam victims all the time: "What is this charge? I didn't buy this!"

And then there was the matter of pricing. There's a scene in the old sitcom *I Love Lucy* where Lucy and Ethel go to an employment agency looking for jobs.

The man asks, "What kind of jobs are you looking for?"

Lucy says, "What kind of jobs do you have open?"

The man replies, "It depends—what kind of jobs can you do?"

Lucy pauses, looks at Ethel, then looks back at the man: "What kind of jobs do you have open?"

And it continues on in a loop until the man screams in exasperation.

Lee and I employed a similar approach in those early days when discussing pricing with potential customers:

"How much does it cost?"

"How much do you have to spend?"

"What's the ballpark range on subscriptions?"

"Well...what's your budget?"

This might sound familiar to early-stage companies trying to find their footing with pricing. We wanted to get as much money as we could from every customer. But at the same time, Lee wanted to build a consistent, defensible pricing structure because he knew marketers talk to one another, and he didn't want to get a call asking, "Why are we all paying different prices?"

BI's pricing was per seat, but Lee had his eye on what he called "the benefiting population." A big tech company might have only three seats accessing the database, but they'd be funneling the profiles to a salesforce of 500. Logically, that company should pay more than one with three seats and just five salespeople. Some customers didn't want to pay for access to the whole database—they wanted to pay for the sliver of information relevant to them.

The complications were stacking up. Nobody wanted to pay for profiles that were available to their competitors, and nobody wanted to wait months to have profiles built if they ordered hundreds at a time. Other prospective customers needed profiles beyond our Fortune 500 offering, and if we didn't have them? No sale—they weren't going to sign on unless we could provide everything they needed. So we offered to produce profiles on demand but couldn't charge for additional work. To make the sale, we'd have to agree to one price and be willing to produce an unknown number of extra profiles as part of that cost. This meant we took on all the risk of someone ordering an avalanche of new profiles, and when one of our software customers started ordering 20 profiles every day for weeks, then months, it was a nightmare.

Lee envisioned how to solve all of these problems. Tracking customer usage, he wanted to plug that data into a framework to carve out subscription levels based on usage to calculate a fair price. BI's growth required modeling subscriptions and formulating pricing. But our database had been built in PHP, a programming language that had now been eclipsed by more modern technology and was now being maintained by a guy in Texas referred to us by Matt Manning. He was a great guy—hard-working, honest and responsive—but he had a full-time gig and there was only so much he could get done. We didn't have the money to invest in the proper site overhaul that would give us the flexibility to track customer usage and refine our business model. Without the functionality to carve up the database and offer information à la carte, dollars were slipping through our fingers as those clients walked away. So we just kept limping along.

CHAPTER TEN
Side Hustler No More

AROUND 2012, Boardroom Insiders began to gain some traction, requiring more of my attention—we'd advanced from limping along to a steady crawl. For four years, I'd been working two jobs—maintaining my consulting gig while fulfilling my dream, building BI. I was also raising two kids, and my consulting clients were demanding more and more of my time. I needed the consulting money to pay the bills—and I was still snapping up C-level projects so I could learn on my client's dime, helping me to position BI in the marketplace while exposing them to BI's capabilities. But I was working every weekend and staying up late every night to do both jobs, and our growth level at BI just wasn't what I'd hoped. I had to face the fact that the business was suffering without my full-time devotion. The words of Michael Blend and Bobby Martin were ringing in my ears: "You've got to focus 100 percent on BI. That's the only way it's going to work."

Something had to give.

My consulting clients treated *everything* as urgent. It even invaded my subconscious. One night, I dreamed I was working in a large room with enormous double doors on one end, like a church sanctuary. I could hear a commotion outside, so I ran to the doors and threw my weight against them to keep them from opening. But they busted open anyway, and a crowd of marketing women rushed in shouting things like, "We *need* it *now!*" "It's *urgent!*"

I thought of scaling up my consultancy by hiring people and starting an agency. I could serve as the face of it, and the hired consultants could do the work under my guidance while I continued to build Boardroom Insiders. But if I did that, the work would never end. I remember telling one of my clients that I'd be working until I was dead. She told me I was so good at it, I'd probably still get work after I was in the ground. I had an image of a client knocking on my coffin, saying, "We have this great opportunity we're hoping you can help us with...and it's *urgent!*"

Working both jobs also cut into what little family time I had. Most of my friends didn't really understand what Boardroom Insiders was or what I was trying to do with it. When the first website launched back in 2008, I was on a weekend getaway with a bunch of other moms I'd met through my kids' school. Whenever I'd break away from the fun to check on the launch, the other moms would good-naturedly chide me about working too much. I was okay with their teasing—most people outside the business world don't understand its pace and that as a business owner, I had to work constantly—on weekends, and even when I was on vacation.

Every year, Andrew, the kids and I went to a family camp at Yosemite for a week. We'd sleep in cabins and gather for group meals with other families in the dining hall, take dips in the lake and pool, and play card- and board games. The week was an annual highlight for years, but the camp didn't have internet access or cell service. It was unthinkable that I could spend a week completely unplugged, so once or twice a day, I'd bike up to a neighboring lodge to check my email. If the lodge's Wi-Fi wasn't working, I'd drive 45 minutes to the nearest town, sometimes with a group of dads—all executives or sales guys—who also needed to check in. It seemed that employers just couldn't leave their vacationing employees in peace for one week of camp. Even with no internet or cell service, they would track 'em down. One morning as I entered the dining hall I noticed a message scrawled in Sharpie taped to the door:

LUCAS HALL:
CALL THE OFFICE ASAP!
IT'S URGENT!

That same week, I witnessed another dad talking on a company-provided satellite phone while pulling a wagon piled with beach towels and inflatables, reachable even while lounging with his family by the camp's lake.

As Boardroom Insiders developed and demanded more of my time, I was always preoccupied, even on regular weekends— squeezing in an hour or two between meals and after bedtime. Andrew and the boys accepted that I loved my work, but people outside my family judged my priorities in a way that didn't seem to happen with working dads.

Happy to be the stay-at-home dad who did freelance work on the side, which wasn't unusual in San Francisco, Andrew *loved* taking care of the boys and the house, and it allowed me to work like crazy. He shuttled the kids around and hung out with other parents at the nearby Starbucks, went on playdates and outings in the local parks. Our family's social calendar revolved around the kids, but I wasn't always able to participate. Depending on what was going on with work, I was sometimes unable to dip into the social scene for several weeks at a time.

I'd hear little comments here and there; one parent even thought Andrew was a single dad.

One evening, I was spending time with some friends, who were discussing a controversy around kids' soccer fields in the city.

"What's all this about the soccer fields now?"

One of the moms turned to me, wide-eyed, and blurted, "How can you have kids in the city and not *know* about this!?"

"Oh right," I faltered, "I think I read something about that in—"

"Seriously, Sharon, where have you *been*?" Another mom, just as judgmental. And these were my friends.

I took a sip of wine, pondered their reaction, and changed the subject. I felt embarrassed and clueless for a few minutes, then my inner voice said, *Really? Who gives a fuck?*

But it put me in a bad mood for the rest of the night.

One Saturday, Andrew took the kids to a friends' garage sale in the neighborhood. I wasn't working that day and had scheduled a spa day with a girlfriend. When an inquiring mom asked where I was and Andrew told her, her sarcasm said it all: "Wow! *That* must be nice!"

We got comments like that all the time. Even in ultra-progressive San Francisco, gender roles were still firmly entrenched.

Having a career and becoming the main breadwinner was a very intentional decision on my part. After my first son was born, I tried being a city mom for a short time while I was on maternity leave. Many moms I knew chose not to go back to work after they had their first kid, and I was curious to know how that felt. Trying to wrangle a group of moms together took too much coordination, so I would just throw our stuff into the car and take off to a park, a museum or some other kid-friendly place. One day, I set up a blanket under a tree, near a playground in Golden Gate Park. My son was an infant, but it was fun watching the older kids run around and climb on things. I brought snacks and figured I'd spend the day reading the *New York Times* and napping with the baby. The weather was beautiful, and I fed my kid and changed his diapers. Nearby, a big group of moms with their babies were deep in conversation:

"What does he eat?"

"I was feeding him store-bought organic food, but it didn't seem right, and his poop looked...odd. So I started making my own baby food..."

"Oh my god, the same thing happened with *us*! Where do buy your produce?"

"Farmer's market, of course!"

Giggles.

"...well, she hasn't been sleeping, and the doctor said..."

Blah, blah, blah, blah, blah.

Holy baby shit, the conversation continued along these lines for more than an hour. I became so agitated, I couldn't even concentrate on what I was reading. Was I a bad mom for not wanting to listen—much less talk about—the minutiae of my baby's diet, poops and sleep habits?

That was it for me. Trial over. I didn't want to be a city mom. I came home and told Andrew I couldn't do it. I was going back to work, no matter what.

I adore my kids, but I continued to be pretty hands off as they became more independent and could do more for themselves. I thought my sons would become who they were without a lot of intervention on my part—kind of like I did. Did that make me a bad parent? A voice in my head sometimes asked, "Why aren't I like the other moms? Should I be doing more?" It's fine with me if someone wanted to dive into parenthood and devote all their time being the best parent they could be, and sometimes I felt guilty for not making that choice, even though I knew the decision I'd made was the right one for me.

I had to spend a lot of time on the road for work, and it

wasn't easy being away from Andrew and the boys, but I think we all enjoyed the breaks from each other. I liked our home quiet and clean, so when I left, it gave them a chance to have a bunch of people over and run amok. At a party, one of my friends pulled me aside and whispered, "I dropped by while you were gone, and I've never seen your kitchen like that. Dirty dishes were piled up all over the place!" I knew there was a frenzy of cleaning before I returned home. I imagined the three of them texting, "MOM HAS LANDED!" and a mad scramble to clean up as I headed home from the airport.

Andrew usually had flowers waiting. Having him as a stay-at-home dad allowed me to commit to my work. I never truly worried about my family because he loved taking care of everyone and making a good life for us.

I discussed quitting my consulting gig with Andrew and the boys as we ate dinner outside at an Airbnb somewhere near Lake Tahoe. They all encouraged me to quit consulting and focus completely on BI, once and for all. My men told me to go all in on my dream.

"You should do it." As always, Andrew had the utmost faith.

"Well…it's a little terrifying, financially."

The boys raised their eyebrows. "Are we gonna go broke?" my eldest asked. Andrew shook his head reassuringly.

"Nah. It'll all work out."

"*How* do you know?"

"Because it always does." His confidence gave me courage.

I had grown to resent consulting because it was taking time away from my dream of building BI. Seeing how much money big companies spent for ideas that went nowhere while my little startup was starving for resources was no longer tolerable. Now that BI was more stable and viable than it had ever been, I ripped off the Band-Aid and quit my side hustle.

The timing was good. By the time I'd made my decision, BI was percolating and starting to gain real traction. We were no longer ahead of the market: executive engagement and C-suite selling had gained momentum. And we were poised to snatch up all the business. Throughout my years of consulting, I had an insider's vantage point in big tech. I sat in on meetings nearly every day, listening to their strategies and challenges. I built trusted relationships with accomplished marketers and worked with amazing mentors, like Mary and Paolo. My business acumen and presentation skills grew sharper. I spent years refining the frameworks and templates that we would turn into software at BI. I had my finger on the pulse of where these companies were headed, and I was introducing them to concepts that could take their sales to the next level—with deliverables that were central to BI.

But surprisingly, it was a tough sell getting my consulting clients to buy into BI—if I wasn't going to do their slide decks, they didn't understand how I could help them. And when they finally did, they had major sticker shock. They thought of me as a hired gun, and all of a sudden I'm asking five to six figures a year for a subscription license. The trick was having Lee lead the negotiations. They had no previous relationship with him, no preconceived notions of his rank or position. He started closing more and more of these deals, and both of us worked our tails off making sure customers got value out of their investment. Things were happening.

And so the transition was complete, with Lee and I leading Boardroom Insiders directly into the barrel of the wave. Things were moving fast: We launched "the box." We started paying ourselves consistently for the first time since BI was formed. And we hit the magical $1 million mark in annual revenue, which everyone said made us bona fide.

Even with these wins, over the course of several years, Lee and I remained at glass-half-empty. We were very critical of ourselves and our business—always looking to make things better. It's the kind of thinking that drives my kids crazy:

acknowledging what's good, then immediately calling out what needs to be improved. But I think that's what made us successful.

Lee was closing deals, so we knew we were on solid ground, with an attractive value proposition that more and more companies were subscribing to. Our renewals were steady as well—by then we had over a dozen solid customers who'd been with us for years, companies like Salesforce, VMware, CA, Adobe and Dell.

What we lacked was a compelling story about the payoff of C-suite engagement. The return on investment. Because we didn't have hard numbers from customers, we defaulted to our standard claim: that C-suite selling helps companies "close bigger deals faster." We had plenty of customer anecdotes to support it, but no one who'd gone on the record with specific figures. It was something Lee had to talk around all the time, and he had gotten really good at it.

But one day in 2016 was a game changer.

Marc Benioff, the CEO of Salesforce, was one of my long-time role models. In 2010, he wrote a book called *Behind the Cloud*, which featured a chapter dedicated to the power of C-suite selling. I blogged about it, but at the time, nobody seemed to be interested in C-suite selling except him...and me. That all changed when I sat down to read Salesforce's quarterly earnings call transcript in early 2016. They'd had a killer quarter, closing a bunch of nine-figure deals, which at the time was phenomenal for SaaS. The analysts were dying to know how Salesforce did it. Marc Benioff replied, "Easy. We sell directly into the C-suite."

I could have done a backflip off my couch.

I thought of the pain of the double sell, the guy at Xerox who didn't care if someone played golf, the executives and VCs who said C-suite selling can't scale. I thought of everyone who had said no until that holy grail of a day when I finally heard Marc Benioff say *yes. Hell* yes.

After celebrating alone in my living room—which involved jumping up and down, pumping my fists and screaming *"I knew it! I knew it!"*—I immediately sat down and excitedly hammered out a blog post:

On a February 2016 earnings call, Salesforce execs crowed about having "the absolute best quarter we have ever had," capping off "a breakthrough year." Management attributed this "amazing success" to "an all-time high in the number of large transactions," including a net-new nine-figure deal, a nine-figure renewal and more than 600 seven-figure-plus transactions.

WOW.

As Vice Chairman, President and COO Keith Block put it, "no one in enterprise software is developing more strategic relationships right now than Salesforce." Salesforce Founder, Chairman and CEO Marc Benioff went on to share the company's secret sauce, a simple and straightforward formula that he says differentiates his company from his competitors and is expanding Salesforce's market share "at the expense of legacy brands like Oracle and SAP."

He sells directly to CEOs.

"When I look at the largest transactions...every transaction was done with the CEO," Benioff said. "I think it's really unusual, and that's why we're really selling more enterprise software than Oracle or SAP."

From then on, I wouldn't shut up about Salesforce. I finally had the kick-ass data points I needed, directly from the mouths of the company's top two executives. And I always managed to add that Salesforce was a longtime Boardroom Insiders customer.

Soon after, the CEO of Adobe—another longtime client—talked about the financial benefits of C-suite selling on their earnings call. *Yes!* I could now credibly go into the marketplace and say, "C-suite selling is critical to big software deals. Both Shantanu Narayen of Adobe and Marc Benioff of Salesforce have called out the value of C-suite selling on earnings calls, and both companies leverage BI to support authentic C-suite engagement."

It gave me so much confidence. I'm not a bullshitter. I want to be able to defend everything I say with facts and data. Finally, I had the fodder to go out and proudly bloviate about BI to everyone, everywhere. And I did.

CHAPTER ELEVEN

BI 2.0

BOARDROOM INSIDERS TOOK flight in 2017. The stats shared by Salesforce and Adobe—along with their testimonials on C-suite sales—had companies banging down our door. We needed to get bigger, fast.

Though we formed our partnership in 2010, our staff remained bare bones in 2017. Other than the single salesperson we hired in 2016, BI consisted of Lee, me and Melanie—who'd worked for us as a contractor for several years before she finally came on full-time. Melanie had worked for Bobby, Lee and Wil at First Research, and when I first hired her as a freelancer, she was a new mom looking to work from home so she could be near her newborn. I was happy to accommodate her—recalling my own desire to work from home years ago when my kids were small.

Melanie was the Swiss Army knife any startup would be lucky to find. A certified public accountant who'd worked for one of the big four, she was also a crack researcher and editor, willing to fill the gaps as our editorial demand ebbed and flowed. For a startup like ours, she was a godsend, though she made it known that when the time was right, she'd prefer to hand off her accounting duties and pursue the editorial track.

Lee had brought in Wade as his first salesperson in 2016. The younger brother of one of Lee's neighbors, he worked out of Lee's tiny office in South Carolina. He'd met Wade at a neighborhood charity bourbon-tasting event, and they hit it off. Wade was pretty young—26—but he had some agency experience and showed a ton of potential. At first, we didn't even have an office for him—he worked out of a conference room where Lee rented a one-man office. He struggled for a good six months before making any sales, but he was doing everything right, so Lee and I knew he would eventually succeed.

Now that Lee had Wade reporting to him, he needed to define the sales process so that Wade could confidently meet with customers without Lee looking over his shoulder. Lee mentored him very closely, and they genuinely liked each other. His first week on the job, Lee took Wade to New York on some sales calls. They had lunch together and would work out regularly at the Y, a short walk from the office. After a few months, Wade just blossomed. I could see his confidence almost physically transforming him. It was beautiful to behold.

Then we hired our first marketer, followed by a research editor fresh out of college, in 2017, and brought Melanie on full-time to focus 100 percent on editorial and help manage our growing team of editorial freelancers and full-time employees. She would prove to be a linchpin for Boardroom Insiders.

As we staffed up in sales and editorial, most of our hires were new grads or just a couple of years out of school. On the editorial side, candidates were required to take a test—and it wasn't easy. I had journalists with years of experience who couldn't complete the assignment, while a Montessori Middle School teacher, who I almost didn't even call for an interview, hit it out of the park.

Melanie blossomed as a manager and loved mentoring the entry-level editorial freelancers. We spent a lot of time discussing individual members of the team, where they needed to improve, what motivated them, and strategizing about how to improve their skills, build their confidence and develop them into leaders. Ambitious Gen Zers and Millennials want to be promoted quickly, and some of the people we hired were eager to prove themselves. When I saw someone excelling, I made sure to acknowledge their achievements before they even knew what hit them. That's where our shock-and-awe employee management strategy came into play.

One of our hires was a young woman named Anna who had a passion for all things HR. The editorial position we hired her for didn't involve HR work at all, but she developed her knowledge on her own time, enrolling in an online course through Northwestern, while still doing great work on the editorial side. Just a few months in, she volunteered to organize and run our internship program and did a wonderful job. In the process, she recognized that we had very little in the way of HR at BI—we lacked the structure and tools that a growing company like ours really needed, like onboarding programs and materials—so as Anna built out the internship program, she proactively repackaged everything for onboarding general new hires. It was great timing, because BI doubled in size that year.

Melanie, Lee and I spent a lot of time contemplating Anna's role. She was smart and ambitious, but her real passion was elsewhere. So we figured we had a choice: we could get some great work out of her in editorial for about six months and have her move on, or we could find a role that she was more passionate about—which would also solve some of our own growing pains. We came up with a proposal, and Melanie and I prepared to present it at her biannual performance review.

"Anna, you've done such a fantastic job with the internship program."

"Wow...thanks." A shy smile. "It's my pleasure. HR is my hopeful career path."

I smiled and looked at Melanie.

"You're terrific at editing, Anna," Melanie chimed in, "but we noticed you really shine when you're taking on the HR side of things."

"Aw, thank you!"

"So what I was thinking…" I paused. Anna really beamed when we talked about HR, and I couldn't wait to drop my idea on her.

"…is that we need someone to take over our recruiting. I used to handle it, but I just don't have time anymore. We also need someone to manage onboarding, training materials…In fact, your interest and the great job you've done have made us realize the need. So thank you."

"Okay…"

Then came the big smile.

"I want to put you in the role of HR manager—halftime to start—while continuing your editorial responsibilities the other half of the time. As long as it all works out, when we grow into the need for a full-time HR person, you can transition into that role."

The look on her face said it all. She was glowing, overjoyed that both her efforts and her true talents had been recognized. (She'd be even more overjoyed later when the transition came with a considerable raise.)

She sat quietly for a few moments, stunned, looking back and forth between Melanie and me.

Then she said, "Well, I came in here with a full page of notes, but I guess I'll just throw them away!"

And that's how the shock-and-awe people management strategy got its start. If I knew someone wanted and deserved something, I did my damnedest to give it to them before they could even ask for it. As long as the company was doing well, we rewarded our employees with unexpected but well-deserved bonuses and raises—communicating what they were doing well and challenging them with goals for the next six months. The stretch goals kept them engaged and ensured they were always challenged—never bored or stagnating. For years, our staff retention rate stayed above 90 percent.

Because we hired and invested in great people, I didn't have a lot of experience reviewing underperformers. It was scary giving negative feedback—I don't like making people feel bad and was acutely aware that most of our new hires were just a few years into adulthood. I remembered what that felt like—trying to get your footing in your first job, when one small criticism could shake your confidence before you'd had time to acquire any. I still hadn't forgotten the day I disappointed Ginny all those years ago.

I'd also think of my own boys.

"I'm about to give bad news to someone's little boy," I said one morning as I prepared to give a negative review and deliver an ultimatum to one of our employees.

Lee rolled his eyes and laughed.

"We *are* running a business after all, Sharon. Henry is an adult. He needs to hear it."

We met over Zoom. Henry looked nervous, and I started backpedaling in my mind.

Stay strong and be fair, I thought.

But, oh geez—look at this poor kid, came my counter-thought. I took a deep breath.

"Henry, you worked really hard to get this job. You had your references call me before I even had a chance to call them. You were really gung-ho."

A nod and a mumble. Henry was waiting for the other shoe to drop.

"But based on your work since then, I'm wondering whether you want to *keep* this job. Because frankly, we can't tell if you're even working half the time."

His face clouded over, and I could tell this was hitting him hard. I saw his Adam's apple jog as he gulped and tried to remain calm.

"We still think you have the ability to do great work. If you'd like to stay, we're willing to see it through—but you're going to have to make some really big changes. Right away."

Finally, he spoke. "I love working at Boardroom Insiders. I really do. I...I guess I just needed a kick in the butt."

We sketched out an improvement plan and at the end of the talk, he thanked me, and his work immediately improved.

I was elated. When I shared the news with Lee, he just smiled and nodded.

Another new hire had amazing business acumen and could parse earnings calls like nobody's business, but he couldn't stop making typos. Meaningful typos. This went on for a while, and it was causing Melanie a lot of extra time in the editing process.

Melanie and I met with him.

"You do the hard stuff really well. You're so good at reading earnings calls and getting all the important analyses done. It's the easy stuff you're messing up, and it's a problem because it takes time for Melanie to fix it."

When he realized the impact his mistakes were having, he worked extra hard to turn his performance around. And he succeeded. Melanie later promoted him, and he became a leader in the company, despite his young age. When we gave him the unexpected news in his review about his promotion and a significant raise and bonus, we were so excited—we were practically crying! I knew how close he was to his family—his mom, in particular.

At the end of his review, I said, "Make sure you call your mom and tell her the news."

We made a point of figuring out what motivated people and what they really cared about. And we used it—not just for our own ends, but to make everyone's job more rewarding.

While there is much fodder about the entitlement of Gen Z,

I saw the opposite in our employees: they seemed to underestimate their own abilities and strengths. That triggered me, as I'd always done the same. So I set out to build them up, not keep them scared or insecure. The risk of successfully developing and empowering people was that they'd become more confident, dream bigger and leave our small company. But I'd always tell Melanie, "If they leave, they leave. If they go on really good terms, it'll be good for them and for us, because when they gain power and influence, we'll have fans and friends in high places!"

We ended up creating loyalty, and we grew leaders who would help us run the company when BI expanded. Developing and rewarding people and watching them shine was the best part of my job.

The people part was fun. But in 2018, Lee and I realized that we needed to do something about the BI website as well. It needed enhancements, but the brittle and now antiquated PHP code the developers in India had built it on was unstable. The site looked really bad, and it was the face of our company. Both of us being non-technical, Lee and I were hamstrung to find strong development partners. But we finally had the money to hire a new firm to rebuild our home page.

Lee and I went to the office of a company called Cloud Castle and met with a bunch of guys around a big table. They were impressive and had a grand vision for our product. We asked them to send us a proposal. And did they ever: to rebuild and maintain our website, they wanted $1 million plus 10 percent of our company! We had just under $2 million in annual revenue. I blew my stack. I wanted to get them on the phone and tell them they had a lot of nerve, but Lee diplomatically turned them down, and we ended up hiring a smaller company who signed on to do the work for a tiny fraction of Cloud Castle's bid.

It was a horrible experience. The new agency sold us on their A-team, then gave us the C-team. Lee and I had to do all the project management and testing, writing out everything that broke, in a long list of bugs to fix. When we'd test the updates, we'd find a bunch of new bugs, along with others they still hadn't fixed. Despite this arduous process, they eventually did deliver a much-improved home page and filtered search, which added stability and new functionality to our site. And because they screwed it up so badly, we got what was probably a $50,000 enhancement for just $13,000. But the process was a scathing pain, and we were without a tech partner once again.

Then one day Lee called me in California to tell me that three of the guys from Cloud Castle left to start their own company, now called Dualboot Partners, and they asked Lee if they could make another pitch to work with us. The guys had all been founding managers. I blew my stack again.

"*What?* The same guys who asked for a million dollars and 10 percent of our company? And they want us to be their first customer? That'll be the day!"

I could hear Lee's wry smile over the phone as he waited patiently—as was his practice—for me to finish ranting.

"Sharon, I think they're sincere. There's no reason to say no."

"I'm not doing business with those clowns!"

"Sharon...Trust me on this one. We should take the meeting."

By now, I completely trusted Lee's judgment. He'd never let me down. So I flew east to meet with the principals of Dualboot Partners.

Todd, Ben and Daniel came to our little office in Fort Mill. They led in by apologizing for the outrageous Cloud Castle proposal and hinted that that kind of approach was part of the reason they'd left. Then they explained that they were connected with offshore developers.

"Whoa. Hold on a second. My last experience working with an offshore web developer was an absolute nightmare."

Lee shot me a look. I shot him one right back. I was standing firm on this one.

The chief technical officer chimed right in: "Our approach is a little different. Our offshore partners are tightly managed. I guarantee the experience will be invisible on your end."

"Put that in writing, and we might have a deal."

Once we were over that hurdle, the CTO took the reins. He was brilliant. Not only did he get what we were saying, he immediately responded with solutions to problems we didn't even know we had. As non-technical founders, Lee and I didn't know what we didn't know, so it was important for us to describe in detail not only the functionality we needed but also how our teams worked. The CTO proposed solutions that would be invaluable to our processes—saving our editorial team a ton of time and tedious work—and they came up with a long list of new ideas for making our processes even more efficient.

The meeting was inspiring, and I told them on the spot that we wanted to work with them.

As with Matt Manning's firm in India, we were once again signing up to be someone's first customer. Putting our content in the hands of a brand-new company to integrate custom software was a risk, but I knew if we succeeded together, it would be a game changer for BI. Was it possible that after a decade, we'd finally found the right development team?

Dualboot matched us up with a two-person coding team in Russia, 600 miles outside of Moscow. Lee and I were so busy that we didn't have time to sit down and brainstorm. So we decided to meet in Park City, Utah—halfway between San Francisco and South Carolina—to nail down our priorities. In the middle of our visit, we got a call from Dualboot: they'd done a deep evaluation of our site's code and they wouldn't be able to retrofit it; to make it right, they'd have to completely recode it in a different programming language. An updated code base would allow us to deploy new features faster, and make quicker fixes, they explained. But it would mean spending another $35,000. Ouch. But we knew it was the right thing to do, considering the original site was built ten years ago with an aging programming language.

Once the site was rebuilt, we saw immediately how much better it was—it was significantly faster, and tweaking or adding features took only a couple of days, as opposed to weeks. The surprising challenge was getting our editorial employees on board. While the changes to the editorial interface on the back end would make their work faster and easier, the rollout did not go well...thanks to yours truly.

In my excitement to get the new system into the team's hands, I swashbuckled—pushing it live the day before Thanksgiving, without bothering to set expectations that there'd be some bugs we'd need to work out. Melanie and two of our editors were still at work when suddenly, with little context or training, they were expected to figure out a new system under pre-holiday deadline pressure. They were stressed...and livid. Not a great way to send your employees off for the holiday.

I quickly recognized my mistake and the downside of being a swashbuckler. Determined to make things right by Monday, I worked with the developers that Thanksgiving weekend to debug the system. Despite having to work over the holiday, I was having a total blast. By Saturday, we had the system working bug-free, and I built out a prototype record so I could be ready to train the team on the power of the new system on Monday. I was energized and thrilled, and I assumed everyone else would be too.

I gathered the team on Monday and walked them through the prototype record, showing them the transformational improvements and new functionality.

"Isn't it incredible? It's going to save you guys so much time! And no more tedious, repetitive tasks."

I looked around at my editorial team.

Stony silence. Zero enthusiasm.

Were they sluggish coming back from the long weekend? Or was this the cold shoulder?

"Melanie, what do you think?"

She uncrossed her arms and moved her head from side to side, like she was loosening up to haul off and bap me one.

"It was really bad on Wednesday, Sharon."

Big pause. The whole team was waiting for my reply. They'd been so traumatized that they had no faith it was going to be as easy as I was saying it was. The rocky rollout had hurt my credibility and put unnecessary stress on my team. It was time to own my shit.

I nodded my head and looked each team member in the eye before I spoke.

"I know...you're right. I messed up. In my excitement, I wasn't thinking about how this would impact all of you in the moment. I should have waited. I'm sorry."

Like a wave washing over them, body postures and facial expressions softened, and they leaned in to look at the new features.

After a couple of weeks, everyone got used to the new system—and loved it. Our Dualboot developers were like ninjas, making additional tweaks requested by the team right away, fixing new bugs as quickly as they were discovered. This gave our team confidence. They could see improvements being made by the hour, and they were posting and celebrating these updates on Slack.

"Hey y'all: it looks like the company filter is working now!"

"Man, I can't believe the amount of time we're saving with searches!"

"Holy crap—this is incredible!"

The developers had earned their respect. And I knew we'd made the right decision on becoming Dualboot's first customer. They really came through.

But there were more speed bumps ahead. The India research

team had a hard time getting up to speed on the new system, and suddenly it was Fort Mill versus India, with our South Carolina team growing increasingly frustrated that India wasn't using the new system correctly.

I called the key team members into a conference room.

"Look, guys...we're about to hire a kid out of college, and we're bringing in more and more new people. If they see you freaking out, they're going to freak out too. And they're going to think this nonsense is okay. It's not."

I glanced around the room at their faces. And that's when I realized I wasn't blameless in all of this. I had to deliver another comeuppance...to myself.

"The truth is...you're following the tone I've set. And I'll own that. But we've got to move on. We're a different company now, and we're all setting the tone."

A few nods and some deep breaths.

"We're going with this new system, and you need to handle it. If you need my help addressing something with India, let me know."

"You got it, Sharon."

"Great. Can we send you a list of items that need attention?"

"Let's hammer them out right now."

Back when Boardroom Insiders was just me, Lee, and Melanie, I would jokingly complain or roll my eyes about drowning in new orders—moan dramatically about vendors being late or things going wrong in the office. When the company was small, I didn't see myself as a boss; I saw myself as a peer. We were all in the same boat. But now that I was the CEO of a fast-growing company, my role had changed and I needed to adjust to that—to set an example and set the tone for the whole firm. Once I owned up to that, the problems disappeared.

On the customer side, it was another story. The enhancements were pretty invisible. Dualboot had rebuilt the entire app in modern, flexible programming language and made major productivity and UX improvements on the back end. It's like we rebuilt a rickety old house in the same footprint, to look exactly the same, but the new house was nicer, safer and more energy-efficient, with double-paned windows. And I got to thinking. When I saw how well Dualboot had delivered, I started plotting a major addition to our "house," one that would put us in a completely new league.

When you work with tech marketing organizations, it doesn't matter that you have an easy-to-use, self-service product that delivers 90 percent of what your clients want. They'll always have special projects that require custom work and plenty of dumpable budget dollars to pay for them. We'd been successfully moving away from custom work toward the subscription model, to boost our ARR.

But at the end of 2018 and the beginning of 2019, we were hit with a wave of custom project requests from some of our most prominent customers—all Fortune 100 tech companies. Suddenly, we had commitments for six huge projects—each with a price point between $50,000 and $100,000, with four to six weeks to deliver. It was an astronomical amount of work... and money. We needed a whole new team right away.

In January of 2019, I turned my dining room into a war room, hired a few smart friends I'd worked with in the past and got down to business. I didn't get my dining room back until seven months later.

While Lee and I were excited about the revenue and the opportunity to blow our customers away with our work, we were more excited about the opportunity to finally develop the software I'd sketched out back in 2016—when Lee made a comment about our database that really got me thinking:

"No one has what we have," he said. "No one. They might have this piece of data here, or another piece there but no one has everything in one place like we do."

"That's because no one else wants to buy in on our business model. Humans! They're too expensive and unscalable."

"Right…and wrong," he said. "We need to think about what else we can build with this unique data set—that *is* scalable. Because no one else will be able to do it—they don't have the underlying data."

I grinned, seeing exactly where Lee was going with this.

"And that'll leave the market wide open…to *us*."

I'd pondered what he said for weeks, and the next time I went to Fort Mill, I pulled out an easel-sized pad of paper and sketched out a blueprint for software that would automatically generate custom-project deliverables. I'd been doing them for so long, and of course I knew exactly how our database was structured, so figuring out how to automate the projects wasn't rocket science. But building the software would be expensive, and back in 2016, we had neither the money nor a development partner to build it. So I rolled up the drawings and put them away in a closet in the office.

Now, a few years later, we had a great development partner, a shiny new app firing on all cylinders and a windfall of revenue committed for six custom projects that needed to be completed in the next six months.

"What if," I asked Lee, "we developed our software alongside all these custom projects?"

His knowing smile told me all I needed to know.

It was a golden opportunity.

The project team I had assembled would use our tried-and-true methods and templates, and Dualboot would build the software in parallel. We could run the projects through the software while we were building them by hand and compare the results. If this worked, it would make us much more attractive to not only customers but also potential funders and acquirers.

Besides me and Lee, no one knew what we were up to. The sales team kept selling our database subscriptions, and they were killing it—closing deals with new customers and renewing existing accounts. With all the custom projects on tap, I officially handed off editorial management to Melanie, promoting her to managing editor. Her team steadily grew, and she ran it like a well-oiled machine.

Meanwhile, my dining room was a hive of activity, as we juggled multiple projects, getting them out the door as quickly as possible while feeding them to Dualboot so they could test the software to see if it would replicate the results. As we completed project after project, I presented the work to our clients: showing them their top 50 accounts, with visual maps indicating the commonalities among their target executives and how they mapped to their own executives, the execs' most common hobbies and deep dives into their business initiatives and challenges, supported by recent quotes and so on.

One day I was sitting at my dining room table, presenting one of these decks over Zoom to a new customer, Amazon Web Services. This one made me a little nervous, because AWS—the Jolly Green Giant of the tech industry—is notoriously tough and demanding. The lead executive had his video turned off, and he was very quiet throughout the entire presentation. I wondered if he was even listening, or maybe just not impressed.

"And that's it." I closed the presentation in the usual way, leaving our Boardroom Insiders logo on the screen. "Does anyone have questions?"

My heart was pounding because I didn't know how to interpret the lead exec's silence.

I fidgeted in my seat. *Shit.*

After a few beats, he finally said, "I am sitting here with my mouth hanging open. This is amazing. I have no idea how you even did this."

Just wait until you hear you can do it all yourself—in just a couple of minutes and just a few clicks, with our new software, I thought, smiling to myself.

This wave of custom projects for Amazon, Workday, Adobe, Salesforce and others teed us up perfectly to close bigger deals with our top customers. The content was the same, the templates looked the same and they were paying us a lot of money for something that took four to six weeks to produce. The new software promised to replicate the deliverables, with just a few mouse clicks.

Until now, the problem with our custom project deliverables was that once we handed them over, the information immediately started to go out of date. Our new software allowed subscribers to create as many reports as they wanted, which would be constantly updated in real time as key executives left their roles and new ones came on board. Their reports would always be current, and new executives would be highlighted so they could see what had changed since they'd last accessed the report.

As the new software began to take shape that spring, Lee started thinking about how he would price and sell it.

We were on a call one day when he tried out his pitch: "Hey [customer name], remember that custom project you paid us for last month that cost $75k and took six weeks to deliver? Well... what if you paid us $125k and you could create as many projects as you want, all year long, and you could generate them in seconds—with just a few clicks?"

"And the data was constantly updated in the background, with no extra work on your part?" I practically screamed.

Our whole business was about to change.

CHAPTER TWELVE
Paying It Forward

I WAS FIRED up about our new software, which we called BI Pro, for so many reasons. One was that we could eventually offer value-added services, which would make our subscriptions "stickier," while offering a path to move our best editorial employees into client-facing, subject-matter-expert roles. Many of them already had the skillset and were hungry to do more. All I had to do was train them. I saw that BI Pro would become the linchpin that transformed BI. Not only would it produce an incredible revenue stream, but it would also separate us from anything else on the market. It could also offer a whole new career path within BI that prevented our people from getting burned out and leaving the company.

At a trade show in early summer 2019, we started to seed the market for the software launch. Lee and I did most of the talking and let our salespeople focus on selling the original database product, which they were experts at. The reaction was positive. I was so proud of the work. So, in a classic swashbuckler move, I previewed screenshots of some of the BI Pro dashboards on LinkedIn, teasing the coming release. I knew it would get attention, and it did. And man, was our sales team *pissed*. They weren't familiar with the new software yet and didn't know how to sell it, and here I was putting it in front of all of our customers, who began asking questions.

Wade, who by this time had earned a ton of respect building a great book of business, and our newly hired VP of Marketing, reined me in.

"Sharon, we need to put some processes around these things. When we launch something, we should have a plan..." That was our polite new VP.

Wade was one of our first hires—the lot of whom now called themselves the OGs. "I don't know how to sell this stuff, Sharon! Clients are calling, and it's embarrassing. I don't know what to tell them!"

Of course, I knew this already. And it was time to issue another apology. Deep down, I was surprised my posts had had such an impact. I'd spent so many years broadcasting to radio silence. But things had finally changed. We were now a $3 million company, and I knew then and there that I had to fall in line or I was going to screw everything up.

"Guys: Of course, you're right. My exuberance gets away with me. I'll set up a team meeting, and we'll go over everything. And I'll kick it off with a *grande mea culpa*."

Once the sales team was onboard, BI Pro proved to be the gamechanger we'd been hoping for. Wade closed the first deal in October 2019—before we even had a chance to name or launch the product. The customer, Cisco Systems, had seen the LinkedIn post, and Wade closed them within a couple of days. It was one of the fastest sales we'd ever made.

We had core clients and staff that were the essence of our success, and we developed those relationships even as we outgrew other vendors or certain staff members and had to manage them out of the business. With the company constantly changing, Lee and I were always pivoting, adapting to a new playing field, and along the way learned our own lessons and developed our leadership skills too. We also discovered that sometimes what might seem like a challenge at first could turn into a huge positive.

We were looking for someone to manage our customer relationship management (CRM) and publish content on our website, such as our blog and marketing materials. The best candidate we interviewed by phone was very enthusiastic, and we hired her on the spot. Jody had an impressive resume, and we were eager to have her join us. But her first day at work, she seemed distracted and not very engaged. At the end of the day, Lee and I went out for a drink and talked about it.

"She's not absorbing anything I'm telling her. I don't get it."

"Maybe she's just nervous, Sharon—working one-on-one with the CEO her first day and all…" Lee's pragmatism always made me take a step back.

"But she was so engaged during the phone interview. It just doesn't make sense. She's like a different person. This is a really important position. I think I may have made a huge hiring mistake here."

"Well, the best you can do is talk to her about it. We always give people a fair shake, right?"

"Right…As usual, Lee."

The next day—before I could even broach the subject, Jody walked into my office and closed the door.

"One thing you should know, Sharon: I'm legally deaf."

Ah! The clouds cleared, and everything suddenly made sense. Jody had a special hearing aid she used for phone calls—so she was able to hear me fine during the interview, but in person she often relied on reading lips. On her first day, I sat alongside her to show her how to navigate our website. Sitting side by side, she wasn't able to read lips very well, so she missed a lot of what I said.

"There's a great messaging tool called Slack that makes it easy for everyone to communicate and collaborate—have you guys ever used it?"

"Nope. Tell me more."

This was how we came to use Slack as one of our most critical business tools and culture builders. Her unique needs led us to what became one of the foundations of our growing company culture. Our team loved it and used it all day long. As I was remote most of the time, I really appreciated having this virtual water cooler so I could check in and chat about things other than business. Slack also served as a great morale booster for shouting out team members or announcing work accomplishments. We created a channel called Sales Bell, where the sales team would post closed deals, renewals and new customers. Every time the Sales Bell rang, everyone went off posting high fives, emojis and gifs. We later renamed it "Team Bell," acknowledging that closing deals was a full team effort.

It was 2020 now, and we were closing in on $5 million in ARR. Lee and I were both overloaded with operational headaches that were ancillary to our core business. As the regulatory environment became trickier for data companies, for example, customers were asking us to complete all kinds of paperwork related to compliance and privacy—important tasks I hated doing and, more importantly, didn't feel qualified to do. HR and facilities tasks were becoming burdensome as well. Lee and I began to feel like we were doing everything, but nothing particularly well. We needed someone to handle these operational details, so Lee put feelers out to his network and before long, he told me there was someone I needed to meet.

I flew East and we spent two days with Tony, talking through our business, the operational challenges we faced and what his role might look like. We needed someone to do everything from ordering snacks and office supplies to finding new office space, tightening up our compliance paperwork and privacy policy and helping us figure out how to harness all our data in one place so we could make better decisions. There were two ways we could go: hire a high-end admin type to take direction from me and Lee or hire someone like Tony, who was a highly intelligent, original thinker. He surfaced ideas I'd never even considered, raised questions I wasn't sure how to answer and approached challenges in ways Lee and I marveled at.

He'd worked in operational roles in high-growth venture capital–backed startups. He'd opened and managed international offices, onboarding multiple new employees every week. He pitched us on forming a management team and using a more defined and disciplined process for strategic planning and executing and measuring quarterly initiatives.

Tony was clearly overqualified for us but excited about the opportunity to implement processes and help develop our infrastructure. He didn't mind walking into chaos, and that was precisely what we needed. Like a tattooed Mary Poppins, he liked to come in and work his magic, get everything organized and running smoothly and quietly leave when his work was done.

Also like Ms. Poppins, Tony had strong opinions and didn't hesitate to call out uncomfortable truths. He raised our eyebrows quite a few times in the span of two days—he was *a lot* to behold. Lee and I were exhausted—which was uncommon for us. While we knew Tony was more than we needed in an ops person, we realized his skills would prove crucial in the grueling due diligence process should we need to prepare the company for sale. Prospective buyers had been knocking on our door pretty regularly for more than a year now, and we needed to get our house in order should the right opportunity come along.

After those two days, we were sold on Tony, and he accepted our offer to be our new VP of Operations in May of 2021. From HR conundrums to data privacy regulatory matters, Tony dove in head first and started solving problems right away. Having him onboard was a game-changer.

As the newest member of our leadership team, he imple-

mented a company-wide project aimed at growth and solidi-
fying our infrastructure. This initiative empowered leaders like
Melanie to take 100 percent control of their departments,
including budgets and hiring decisions. She was promoted to
editor-in-chief and given another raise. I was so thrilled and
proud. Mel and I had both started our journey at Boardroom
Insiders with similar goals: to make money working from home
so we could spend more time with our families. How far we had
come! I led a leadership initiative designed to ensure the
company could function without us if Lee and I were hit by a
bus. In just several months, Tony's impact on Boardroom
Insiders made us rock solid from a buyer's perspective.

The "if we get hit by a bus" initiative was a brilliant move. If
we didn't find a buyer and continued doing business as usual,
Lee and I would be freed up to plan and lead the next phase of
the company's growth. Lee called it "working *on* the business
instead of *in* the business." But if the company did sell, our
leaders would be well prepared to own and run their departments, even if Lee and I stepped down. With Tony's support and
leadership, we got an astonishing amount of transformative
work done in the second half of 2021 and were poised to sell.

Despite fears about how the prolonged pandemic would
impact our business, both 2020 and 2021 had been big growth
years for Boardroom Insiders. Our headcount doubled in 2020,
and we were continuing to hire at a rapid clip in 2021. With the
sales team bringing in more deals, our editorial team was
expanding, to the point where it was by far the largest at the
company. Melanie had turned our editors into an efficient,
high-performing group, freeing me up to focus on other things.
Lee and I were aiming to move our daily responsibilities to the
leadership team.

I felt so proud of what we'd accomplished and the employees
we'd nurtured along the way. When I started BI, I had no experience managing people. Now, we had a solid crew we'd devel-

oped who were running their own shows. Along the way, there'd been some tough conversations, but they always yielded the right results. As long as we could see that someone was trying, we gave them time to grow into their role. Hiring was hard, and we would rather work with someone to get them where they needed to be than start over with someone new. We grew attached to people, which made us even more determined to help them succeed.

I often think about the talent we would've lost if we'd behaved like bigger companies and fired people for not performing within a three-month timeframe. We never considered the people we hired to be disposable. If they had the right intent, intelligence and heart, we'd get them where they needed to be. I was always aware of the harm done to someone's life and family when they get fired, and I never wanted to kill someone's confidence. We were focused on a bigger mission than managing people, one that was much more satisfying: we wanted people to transform into confident leaders. Seeing it unfold was the most gratifying experience of my career. I had great mentors when I started out at *San Diego Magazine*, and I was hellbent on paying that tradition forward in their honor.

After getting vaccinated in April 2021, I started traveling to Fort Mill once a month to work with the team in person. While we never fully returned to the office after the pandemic, everyone came in at least two days a week—and after months of being stuck at home, I loved every minute of it. Lee and I had built our own little empire: product and people alike. And we were standing at the threshold of our greatest goal: offers were starting to come in, and there was only one question now: What's the business worth? But there was also one downside— what was going to happen to our bright, shining team when we sold?

CHAPTER THIRTEEN

Getting Our Tires Kicked

IN 2021, Boardroom Insiders won a couple of significant awards. We were included in *Inc. Magazine*'s list of the 5,000 fastest-growing companies. That one was a no-brainer—it was based on math: we had steady growth over three years and the financials to prove it. Then we won a Codie Award for best information product, beating out strong competition, including companies worth more than $1 billion. I was so proud of both awards—their rigorous standards and stellar reputations gave us more visibility and added weight to our marketing campaigns. They also brought more interest from prospective buyers. We were now getting two to three emails a week from bankers and private equity firms, requesting meetings. But taking other people's money would mean giving away a percentage of the company, and we weren't about to give up any equity now.

We were in great shape financially and felt confident that the due diligence process involved with a potential sale would go smoothly. BI now had sufficient ARR to fund the company and pay Lee and me the salaries we deserved after so many years of struggle. He was great at conservatively managing our cash, knowing what was sustainable—whether it was hiring or making an investment like building software with Dualboot. He did the same with our compensation, funding our 401(k) and profit-sharing plans. Lee looked out for us both—always searching for ways to make us whole while adding new employee benefits that would put more money in everyone's pockets. After all those years, we were doing well.

A few years earlier, the question was *if* we could sell. Now it was just a matter of time...and numbers. Valuations were at record highs, and we wanted to get out before the next inevitable market crash. Companies like ours, with an ARR model, typically sold on multiples of revenue. Historically, a typical multiple might be three to six times revenue; but in late 2020 and early 2021, we heard some companies were getting as much as 12 times revenue, which was crazy. We knew we'd never fetch a multiple that high because of our scalability issue and the fact that our product use cases were more niche than universal, but we wanted to take advantage of the frothy multiples, which we knew would plummet with a market crash or a recession.

We worried endlessly about our worst-case scenario: everything crashes, valuations collapse and suddenly we're worth a whole lot less. A recession then drags on and our customers cut budgets, canceling new deals and renewals, leading to a death spiral from which it would take years to recover. If Lee and I were exhausted by success, I couldn't imagine what it would feel like to manage the company through terrible times, making cuts and layoffs. We wanted to go out on a high note.

During the pandemic, we expected that interest in BI as an acquisition would fall off, but that didn't happen. While the early part of the pandemic killed or delayed deals, PE firms needed to do something with their money, or they'd have to give it back to their investors. There was a scramble to find deals. Firms normally looked at companies above $10 million in revenue, but suddenly they started looking at companies with

$5 million in revenue...like BI. To us, clearing $5 million a year was massive, but it was small potatoes compared to other companies. Even Michael Blend kidded us: "Zero to $5 million in 12 years!"

I had a vague notion of how these deals worked, but I wasn't really clear on the players, or what the difference was between private equity firms, M&A bankers and strategic acquirers. And we were hearing from all of them.

The first call or email would usually come from a lower-level representative responsible for generating leads. Their job was to do some initial research on the company and then set up a meeting to determine whether we fit their criteria as a viable acquisition candidate. They look at revenue, type of business, subscriber renewal rate, average deal size, margins, etc. If they decided it was worth another conversation, we'd meet with a more senior decision-maker. This is where the conversation typically ended. We were too small, not scalable or outside of their area of focus. There were a few who wanted to keep talking, so we'd sign a nondisclosure agreement and share financials. We made it to that stage with a few firms.

Private equity (PE) gets a lot of bad press, some of it for good reason. But for entrepreneurs like me and Lee, a PE deal had the potential to deliver a worthwhile exit. A firm might offer to buy 80 percent of a company—meaning that Lee, I, and the other current shareholders would split the cash from the 80 percent purchase, and all the shareholders would retain the remaining 20 percent of the shares. Lee and I would then be paid salaries to run the company for a contracted number of years. As majority owner, the PE firm takes control, defining and overseeing aggressive revenue growth targets: "We want you to get to $15 million in two years," for example. They might decide to combine us with one or more of the other companies they own, fund and help us build out our executive team or provide other forms of support, such as introductions to potential customers.

Being acquired by a PE firm would give us the resources we needed to grow even faster.

The PE firm's exit strategy is typically to sell the company again for a big profit after two to three years of growth. Sometimes this works out great—entrepreneurs I've met who were backed by PE firms were given access to top-level consultants and were able to recruit talented CFOs and operating executives and quickly take their revenue to a new level. Others shared more cautionary tales, including stories of unrealistic revenue targets and relentless oversight of the founders, leading one to describe it as "going from being my own boss to having a constant knee in my back."

Lee and I met with a small PE firm, and the principal shared a story that was hard to forget. He once had a client who owned a road-paving business that contracted with cities and towns. He grew the business to around $10 million or so, but his kids had no interest in taking over the company, so he sold 80 percent to a PE firm at a $25 million valuation, retaining 20 percent of the shares and growing the firm for a few more years—at which time, it was sold again for something like $80 million. Remember, he still owned 20 percent of the shares, so that meant he got a second payout. After that deal, he kept running the company, and a few years later it sold again for nearly $200 million. So he received three big payouts from running and selling the same company three times. In industry parlance, this is having "a second bite at the apple," or, in the case of the road-paving CEO, a third.

I liked to imagine such an amazing outcome for me and Lee —becoming whole with an initial cash payout, then continuing to run the company with a good salary and more resources and connections, and selling it a second time. But we risked a hard knee in our back for that second bite at the apple, and I wasn't sure either one of us could endure that after all we'd been through.

We were also getting calls from companies interested in buying us outright to integrate into their business, though they didn't usually couch it in those terms. Companies that competed with us for client budget dollars or were in an adjacent business typically approached us under the guise of "exploring a partnership"—which usually means they want to learn more to determine whether you'd be a good acquisition target, now or in the future. I always researched the heck out of these companies before a call to see if I could discern their strategy and how we might fit into it. Lee and Michael were more casual about these forays because the majority of partnership conversations go nowhere. "Don't put a lot of work into preparing for these," Michael advised. "They can eat up all your time."

In 2021, we were courted by a San Francisco PE firm. They'd first reached out to me in 2020 during the pandemic, and I agreed to a mask-wearing, physically distanced outdoor meeting at a café near Dolores Park. We signed an NDA and shared our finances, but they decided we were too small and wanted to see a couple more quarters of consistent growth and customer renewals before going any further. So Lee and I decided to keep our heads down and focus on managing and growing the business. Months went by without hearing from them, and we had such a bang-up year in 2020 that we forgot all about them.

One day in April 2021, I was sitting with Lee in our Fort Mill office when they called us out of the blue. They'd passed us over once before, so we weren't optimistic, but we listened to what they had to say.

"Look, we could get you a term sheet for $48 million today."

That got our attention.

"Well, that sounds promising," Lee replied, "let us know what you need from us right now, and we'll think it over."

The instant we got off the call, I looked at Lee. "Holy shit!"

"I know…That's the first time anyone's floated a number."

"I mean, $48 million? Holy fuck!"

We didn't really have a sense of what BI was worth. We'd been maintaining a spreadsheet for years, plugging in different valuations, along with all the deal fees—M&A, accountants, lawyers, etc. We had numbers for every scenario, in increments of $5 million, mapped out to the dollar. Sometimes I'd open up the spreadsheet, stare at it and wonder, "Is this ever going to happen?" We figured the value was somewhere between $20 million and $50 million, but that was a huge delta, and no one had ever floated a solid number…until now.

I jumped up out of my chair and flew out of Lee's office, ducking out into the hallway to be out of earshot of our employees. I dialed Michael Blend, who as usual was driving down a dirt road in Hawaii with spotty cell service.

"They're all full of shit!" he shouted over an audible roar as he drove. "They always throw out a big number to hook you in."

I finally exhaled as Michael resuscitated me with reality.

"It's a game. They want to get you excited—reel you in, then whittle the price way down. It's called 'retrading.'"

"Okay…so, we shouldn't even bother?"

"Well, listen to what they have to say, but…I wouldn't waste much time on it."

So it was a bullshit game, and all the players were 100 percent full of it.

Then Michael asked why we were considering selling. The last time we'd talked, a few months earlier, I told him our success in 2020 had encouraged us to lay low and grow our ARR, to drive a higher valuation.

"If you weren't thinking about selling before, this one conversation shouldn't turn your head," he said. "There will be more offers. You *are* going to sell this company someday. But if you're serious about selling, you need to hire a banker and do it properly. Have them take you to market. Decide if you want to run a process."

When we hung up, I returned to Lee's office and related the entire conversation. "What does he mean by 'a process'?" I asked him. Lee explained that an M&A banker acts like a realtor for companies looking to sell. You wouldn't put your house up for sale and negotiate with one buyer at a time. A realtor evaluates your property, recommends a sale price and the really good ones recommend and even manage improvements and staging to get you the best price. They also develop a marketing plan designed to create interest and competitive bidding.

The work of M&A bankers is not all that different, but the numbers are way bigger. They start by scrutinizing every detail of the business—the financials, the customers, the market, the deal structure, everything. Then they put together a package and send it out to two groups of potential buyers: PE firms that would buy a majority stake, and the "strategics"—companies that have adjacent products and services and would buy outright and integrate us into their portfolio.

Michael's advice was incredibly valuable. Lee and I were convinced an economic crash was coming, and while we didn't feel quite ready to sell, we were both adamant that we needed to get out before the crash. After all the tough times we had already been through, we did not want to find ourselves managing the business through a recession or major tech downturn.

So we decided right then and there to go for it and run a "process."

"Listen Sharon," Lee said. "As the majority shareholder, you have the most to win and the most to lose. So you need to run this thing."

That's how I ended up leading our M&A process. We interviewed three M&A bankers, and all three said our range was somewhere between $30 million and $50 million. I then spent a solid week interviewing 12 different entrepreneurs that the bankers provided as references. I took copious notes so I could share everything with Lee later; it was like a crash course in M&A and due diligence. In my 14 years running the company, those were some of the most valuable conversations I ever had.

On Labor Day 2021, I signed a contract with Leonis Partners out of New York City, and we were off and running.

Michael, usually an optimist, warned me there was a 50-50 chance a deal wouldn't happen, even with a banker.

"*So* many things can go wrong. Don't start counting your money."

Over the course of the next few months, he checked in with me often, even though his own company was about to go public. The conversations were challenging, illuminating and had a big impact on our decision-making as we worked through the deal process. I knew that while Michael's return on his investment in BI could be considerable, it was just a drop in his bucket. But he knew what was at stake for us and continued to be a great friend and mentor.

During September and October, we worked with Leonis to craft our story and create a marketing deck they would distribute to a list of potential buyers. They assembled a list of 150 companies to contact—half of them PE firms, half strategics. Then they worked the phones, calling their contacts at the companies to gauge interest. A shorter list requested our marketing deck, and Leonis set up meetings with a handful that wanted to learn more. While these were called "management presentations," Lee and I didn't present a thing. Despite the high stakes, the meetings were easy, low-stress and, for me, strangely exciting and fun. They already had the most sensitive details of our business in the marketing deck, including our financials, so I didn't feel like we could get tripped up.

In mid-November 2021, just six weeks after we'd started our process, our first offer came in. The good news is that it was a strategic deal, and an all-cash offer, from a company we knew and had met with before. The bad news was that it was well under the $30-50 million range all three bankers had quoted us.

The potential buyer was a UK-based information services business called Euromoney that had been buying up companies focused on "people intelligence." They'd reached out to us a few years prior, but—like all the other partnership conversations we'd had—it didn't go anywhere. Now they had submitted a written offer to buy us outright. Boardroom Insiders would be the fifth company they acquired in the people intelligence category. Two of the other companies focused on researching wealthy people for the benefit of financial services providers and fundraising departments at nonprofit organizations. The other two harvested data on businesspeople, like we did. Euromoney's intent was to combine all five companies into one giant people intelligence business, which they would go on to rebrand as Altrata.

Their first offer was $17 million to $20 million. We were baffled. Why the range? Robert Koven, our lead banker at Leonis, agreed. Did this mean they were really offering $17 million but were willing to go as high as $20 million? Did the higher number represent the negotiating floor? Lee ran the deal terms by some of the people in his network, including one of the bankers we interviewed but didn't hire, who was a neighbor. He told Lee that an all-cash offer was very attractive in the current market, and we should consider it. The deal would be simple from a legal standpoint—we didn't have to worry about earnouts or getting stock in the parent company—and would be quick to close.

While Lee talked to his neighbor, I called Michael to share the news and get his thoughts. He confirmed what Lee's neighbor had said about the all-cash deal: that was the good part. But he also thought the price was too low. It amounted to 4.2 times revenue.

"Well, what's your number?" Michael asked.

"The valuation from all three M&A bankers was $30-50 million!"

"Yeah, but...what's your walk-away number? It's a cash deal. If, say, $25 million is enough, do you walk away at $24 million? You've got to think about that."

The process for arriving at a sales price for BI seemed so arbitrary. Valuations are "squishy" in that they're based on all sorts of variables—some subjective, others that vary wildly from deal to deal. Just because one company sold for nine times ARR didn't mean we could pull off the same. Lee and I preferred to base our decisions on real data, particularly for something so critical to so many people's futures—mine, Lee's, and that of both our families. Our employees also had a stake via a phantom equity plan we set up in late 2020 in anticipation of a sale. Of course, we wanted to get as much money as possible. But how much was enough? While things like financial fundamentals and market size came into play, it really came down to the buyer—how bad they wanted you and what they were really willing to pay.

I pondered Michael's question and sat down to think through the data points that I did have. The $30-50 million range we were quoted by the bankers encompassed all sorts of deals, including those that might include stock and earnouts. So it made sense that an all-cash offer would be at the lower end of that range. I looked at what Euromoney had paid for its other four people intelligence businesses and what those multiples looked like. The fact that it was a public company (and a British one at that) meant that it was likely going to take a more fiscally conservative approach to dealmaking than a public company with a Silicon Valley heritage. I found out that the multiples for its other recent acquisitions ranged from less than one to 2.6 times revenue—not great multiples at all and far below what we were seeing in the frothy marketing technology space. Still,

Euromoney was offering us a 4.2 multiple, considerably higher than any of their other four deals.

Based on all of this information, I figured we weren't going to get much more out of Euromoney. And yet...I was determined to get more.

I called Michael back.

"$30 million is my number."

"Okay, then!" he said. "Go get it!"

We went to our M&A bankers with the $30 million number. I knew it might be a tough conversation, but this was our future we were talking about. We'd worked so hard and underpaid ourselves so many years—there was no way we were going to back down just because we were worn out or fearful. But the additional $5-10 million Lee and I felt we deserved wasn't a big incentive for our bankers—and it meant more work. You'd think: the higher our sale price, the higher their commission, right? While that's true, these guys (and yes, they were all guys) were simultaneously working on deals over $100 million—and working 24/7. So I surmised that the extra $5-10 million—in the context of the other, bigger deals they were handling—wasn't as much of a motivator for them as it was for us. But there was a big risk: if we didn't get the extra money and decided to walk away from the deal, they wouldn't get any commission at all.

So on November 16, 2021, with input from Lee and Michael, I crafted an email to our bankers: "We believe Euromoney is a good fit for our company. Their offer calls out the strategic value that Boardroom Insiders would bring to their people intelligence business and their B2B media strategy. With multiples being what they are for recurring-revenue, subscription-based businesses, we are looking for a minimum of $30 million. A strategic deal at or above that number would be a homerun and an easy "yes" for us. So while we love pretty much everything else about this offer, we are far apart on valuation. We are hopeful [for] a deal that gets us where we need to be and we are asking you to go back to them and negotiate on our behalf."

While this was unfolding, Andrew was consulting with our financial advisor about what the sale would mean for us. While I'm great at hustling and making money, my personal financial acumen is not very high, so I had no clue about what I needed for retirement. I didn't even know if I'd be retired—and wasn't ready yet. I loved working and was hoping Euromoney would keep me on for a while. We had a lot of exciting projects and launches in the hopper, and I wanted to see it all through with the team I loved.

Lee and I discussed what our "walkaway" number was. We settled on $25 million in cash.

And the very next day, that was exactly what Euromoney came back with—a $25 million cash deal!

A few days later, we signed an exclusivity letter agreeing to the terms and attesting that we wouldn't negotiate with another buyer for a period of four weeks.

CHAPTER FOURTEEN
Closing Marathon

SIGNING the letter of intent marked the beginning of the due diligence process, which I had been warned about by other entrepreneurs. "Imagine going to the proctologist," one of them said, "every day for two months!"

Ouch.

Lee and I braced ourselves. We kept good records and used careful practices over the years, managing all of the little details in preparation for this very process. And we had Tony the Fixer. How bad could it be?

Due diligence took about two months. Euromoney brought in their super-smart quant-heads to crunch our numbers and evaluate the quality of our revenue. As Lee predicted so long ago, our custom-project revenue was deemed not "real"—they were interested only in the value of the annual subscriptions. Gaps in renewals were a point for intense probing, and our habit of extending good grace to our loyal customers raised a red flag. Sometimes our bigger customers wouldn't get their paperwork and approvals together to renew subscriptions before they expired; if they told us they intended to renew, we'd keep their accounts open in the interim. And, as it turned out, heralding the fact that we killed it during the pandemic was a double-edged sword: all the budget dumping that occurred during the pandemic—would that revenue go away next year? Lee did a great job answering these questions.

Euromoney's lawyers kept sending requests for documents I'd already shared with them multiple times. I was like a machine and had everything at the ready. "Okay, here you go. Here it is again, here it is again, here it is again." Or they would say, "We know you shared this information, but now we want it in a different format." I fielded these requests all day long, finding and sending more documents, jumping on calls, answering questions. Up until this point, due diligence hadn't been so bad, and I thought we might get through without losing our minds.

On the positive side, Euromoney seemed impressed with how we'd been running the company. We ranked higher than any other acquisition in financial data, security systems, state and federal tax compliance and privacy issues. I credited Lee for all this: he knew that not having every detail in order could tank a deal. And they were blown away by our employee survey results—they'd never seen employee satisfaction this high, anywhere.

As we'd grown, fostering and maintaining a strong company culture and retaining employees was important to us—we wanted to make BI a great place to work, so we put some budget behind it, planning all-company events and giving each department a budget to do fun things, like take their peers from other departments out to lunch or happy hour. We hired a consultant to investigate where Lee and I thought our culture should be in comparison to what our employees actually thought, and we were happy to see that we were closely aligned. Monthly surveys helped us understand how people were feeling about their jobs and the company in real time, and we would pore over the results and obsess about how we could improve.

And we had the foresight to ensure that our loyal employees

would benefit when we sold the company. In late 2020, Lee and I decided to be transparent about our endgame. With everyone able to see our calendars, Lee worried that people would start noticing meetings with M&A and PE firms. In absence of facts, the rumor mill kicks into high gear, so we decided to tell everyone that our plan was to sell BI someday, though we weren't sure when that might happen. And we wanted to show employees that we had a plan to reward their work with a share of the proceeds if we sold.

We worked with our lawyers to put together a phantom equity plan that placed a percentage of net proceeds from the sale in a pool, by which all vested employees would receive a payout, based on seniority and contribution to the business. We unveiled the plan at our last company meeting in 2020. It had become our tradition to unveil a new employee benefit at the end of each year: one year it was our 401(k) plan, the next year a profit-sharing plan. It was part of our shock-and-awe philosophy of rewarding people when they're not expecting it.

We had slides that outlined our goals for 2021: the revelation that we planned to sell, the announcement of the equity plan and an overview of how it worked. After the meeting, everyone had their phantom equity agreement in their inbox. The shock-and-awe method leaves everyone speechless. I saw this time and again in meetings like this and in reviews where we gave unexpected raises and promotions. After we announced the plan, everyone was silent. Nobody asked any questions—it was crickets. I think they needed to sit with it and think about what it meant for them, because it wasn't too long before Lee and I started getting messages in Slack:

"Oh my God! Thank you so much."

"You guys are awesome!"

One sales guy said, "I'm gonna make you guys so much money!"

We agonized over the formula for payouts. Each new hire

got something, but if people left, they lost their share and it went back into the pool. We kept questioning ourselves on the formula dictating who would receive what based on merit and tenure. And as we moved closer to the sale, it hit home how big this was for everyone. And we started getting nervous about revealing all the facts now that a deal seemed imminent. We'd told everyone we planned on selling *someday*, but it seemed that day had come!

From the time we hired our banker to the day before the deal closed, only the leadership team knew about the pending deal. Being a public company, Euromoney insisted we tell no one beyond our leadership team. And we had to be careful about timing the announcement because we didn't want people to get too excited and take their eye off the business. There was always a chance the deal wouldn't close, so we didn't want to get everyone fired up and then let them down if nothing happened.

As the deal grew imminent, Tony did what Tony does—he scrutinized everything, including the phantom equity plan—and found language in the contracts that didn't represent our intention: if an employee left the company, their share of the proceeds would go back to the shareholders, not the phantom equity pool. So we scrambled to redo the contracts. The tricky part was getting everyone to sign the new paperwork without alerting them that a deal was imminent.

It was now Monday, January 17, 2022. I had been in South Carolina for a week, taking care of all the last-minute due diligence requests and waiting for our deal to close. We were supposed to close the previous Friday, but it kept getting delayed. That night, I got a call from Michael Blend, who was about to take his company public the following week, but still made the time to check in with me. I told him that Euromoney was assuring us that we were closing in two days.

"What do your employment agreements look like?" he asked.

"We don't have them yet. They said—"

"What? There's no way you're closing on Wednesday, Sharon. Employment agreements take more than a week to negotiate. Talk to your lawyers—they should be on top of this. They should be *demanding* this."

"Shit. I never considered that, with everything else going on."

Michael continued, "If you close on Wednesday, what are you going to do on Thursday?"

"Wake up and run the company," I replied. "Nothing is going to change immediately, right?"

"Really? Will you have health insurance? Will you be getting paid? You don't know what your deal is. Maybe you're out. You don't know. That has to be defined before you close the deal... and that takes time."

Lee and I had repeatedly asked what Euromoney's plans were for the two of us, and we still didn't know. That should have been a sign. But we'd been buried in due diligence, barely keeping our heads above water. I'd gotten very little sleep over the last two weeks trying to get the deal over the finish line.

I told Lee what Michael had said, and we immediately got our lawyers on the phone. By this time, it was after 8 pm and we hadn't even eaten—everyone was working around the clock to get the deal done.

"So, guys: shouldn't we have employment agreements by now?"

"Yes," the lawyer replied. "It is unusual that you don't have that yet."

"So what's our next step? Why hasn't this come to light before now?"

Considering we were paying our lawyers a $200,000 deal fee, we were disappointed we had to bring this to their attention —at the last minute.

They got on the phone with the Euromoney people, who said they were planning to offer Lee and me consulting agreements but didn't provide any more details. Fine. At least we knew what the intention was.

Monday that next week, we were on the "final" wrap-up call the day before the deal was supposed to close.

"There's one last item. About your consulting agreements—"

"What about them?"

"Well, they'll be for a maximum of three months . We'd like you to step down from running the company right away."

We were totally blindsided. Lee is usually poker-faced on Zoom calls, but I saw the shock register as Euromoney delivered the news.

Tuesday dawned. After a few hours of sleep, Lee picked me up at my hotel and we were driving around Charlotte, discussing the transition and what it was going to be like to say goodbye to our employees and hand over the reins—just like that. At least they'd have the proceeds from their equity deals to remember us by.

That's when my phone rang. It was our lawyer.

"Guys, the buyer's legal team needs us to cancel all those phantom equity agreements with your employees—ASAP."

Silence and shock.

We were dumbfounded.

"What the hell? Are you kidding me!? Why?" I replied.

"They're afraid they might create a potential liability after the sale. You need to cancel them. And it needs to be done today."

I broke in. "What do they mean, 'cancel' them?" They don't want us to pay out our employees? The buyer's got nothing to do with making the payments—they're coming out of our money after the sale. It has nothing to do with them at all!"

"While that's all true, the buyer needs them canceled so employees can't come back to them after the sale and try to make a claim that they were not paid. Gotta get it done today."

"Wait," I said. "My problem is with your use of the word

'cancel' because that sounds like they are not going to be getting their money. They WILL be getting their payouts as long as they are vested. So I think the word you should be using is 'redeemed.' You need those agreements redeemed, not canceled, correct?"

The lawyer agreed. After a few very stressful minutes when I thought he was trying to claw back the money intended for our team, we were finally on the same page.

"Um, okay. But if we redeem the agreements today, the employees are gonna ask why—and we'll have to tell them about the sale."

"No—no, no. You can't tell them about the sale."

I took another deep breath and rolled my eyes at Lee, who was driving us back to the office. Was this guy for real? He was insisting our employees sign paperwork to trigger payouts that they knew would only occur if the company was sold...without realizing that the company was being sold! My employees were too smart for that, and I had no intention of being a part of this scheme. There was no way this was going to fly.

"Well, that's not going to work. We have to tell them *something!*" I reasoned.

A few minutes later, the lawyer called us back with a solution: "redeem" the agreements with all vested employees and tell them about the sale—and ask them not to discuss it with anyone, especially their colleagues. Unvested employees, he said, should be told nothing.

I ended the call and looked over at Lee as we both considered how this would impact our people. This was hugely problematic. Telling half of our employees about a pending sale and not the other half—and asking them not to discuss it with any of their colleagues—was not only unrealistic, it was a complete violation of all the cultural practices and principles we'd worked so hard to build over the years. This was our integrity on the line. It was everything we stood for.

Back at the office, I was distraught...and livid. Lee and I sat there late into the night trying to figure out another way, but we kept coming up short.

At the leadership team meeting the next morning, I updated the group on the deal—closing was imminent. Then I broke the news about the phantom equity agreements: later that day, half of the company would know we were selling, and the other half would be left in the dark. I watched as dismay washed across the faces of our leaders...then shock and disappointment. How could Lee and I allow this to happen? Tony was very angry.

He shook his head. "This is going to be a disaster. No matter what we say, people are going to talk to each other. This completely violates the standard of transparency we've worked so hard to establish! This is out of line."

Lee took a deep breath.

We knew, of course, that Tony was right. We'd both lost sleep last night.

I was upset, frustrated and running on junk food.

"We know. We're fully aware. Believe me, if there were any other way—"

"Sharon and I were up late, looking for another way, and there just isn't one," Lee said.

I was so tired. "It's too ironic. We set out to do something positive for our employees, and now everyone's going to be completely pissed off as a result. And the reality is that we didn't *have* to do any of this."

That's when Tony let loose. "C'mon Sharon! Don't act like you did us any favors by giving us equity. Without that, no one would still be working here!"

He ripped into me. Tony is very passionate—it's one of the reasons I loved working with him: his integrity is also off the charts. He'd only been with us for six months, but he knew the culture inside and out, how much we valued transparency and that we don't bullshit around when it comes to doing the right thing by people.

And so I lost it in front of the whole leadership team. I was devastated—and also pissed. The remainder of that meeting is a blur, but I know that at one point, I said to him, "I think you know exactly what kind of person I am."

This led to an epic breakdown. I was exhausted. I'd been at the office over a week, in meetings until 10 o'clock every night. I hadn't been eating regularly. I was supposed to fly home that afternoon after the deal closed.

And then it didn't.

The closing had been delayed *again*. I just started bawling. I fell apart. Everyone else was silent. Someone pushed a tissue box across the table.

Through sobs, I blurted, "You know me, Tony. You know I wouldn't do this if I had a choice. We looked at every angle, and there's no other way. If you think you can figure one out, go ahead!" Then I blubbered again.

Tony's tone changed, and he shifted into solution mode. "Okay, let's talk this through."

But I couldn't stop weeping. I had to get out of there. I walked into Lee's office, Lee trailing behind me. He waited patiently for me to pull it together, but I couldn't.

"Why are you crying? It's okay."

"I'm crying because I've let *everyone* down...and now I've let you down by crying!"

"Sharon, it's okay. Really, it's gonna be all right."

It was embarrassing to break down in front of my team. It was horrible to cry in front of my partner.

I blew it.

I let everybody down.

We'd tried to do the right thing by our employees. We were almost at the finish line, and the lawyers ruined it—and there was nothing I could do to make it right.

I calmed myself down just enough to keep moving. That afternoon, we had to share the news with 14 vested employees via Zoom because we were closing the next day. Lee and I would each tell seven people. I had to get my shit together.

It was already after 1 pm. I had to leave for the airport by 4, and I hadn't even eaten anything or scheduled my calls yet. I set myself up in a private office, and when Melanie popped in to ask if I needed help working out my script, I started crying again, appreciative of her kindness. Then we were both crying. Watching her grow into such a stellar leader at BI was one of the most rewarding experiences of my career.

The calls ran the full gamut. We were handing out hundreds of thousands of dollars from the pool, on top of the raises and profit-sharing bonuses we distributed earlier in the year—putting more money in their pockets in recognition of the roles they'd played building BI into a great company. And we were thrilled to do it.

One meeting was with an employee who had just fully vested the day before. He couldn't even comprehend what was happening.

"Oh...so I'm not getting the money."

"No! You're getting all of it! You just became 100 percent vested yesterday!"

He was stunned, but happy to hear about his unexpected, five-figure bonus.

For others, it meant paying for their kid's college or making a down payment on a house.

I wanted to share the good news with each person as long as I could, but I had to hop in an Uber to the airport. The closing was scheduled for the next day. I still hadn't eaten, and it was 5 pm.

Of course, my flight was delayed. And delayed. And delayed. The kind of delay where they want you to remain near the gate and won't tell you how long the delay will be, but they keep delaying it again and again, every 20 minutes. I headed to the Admirals Club in search of food and made friends with the concierge. He agreed to page me when the flight was *really* boarding.

With some food in my stomach, I boarded my 6 pm flight around 9 pm. At least I was finally headed home.

But shortly after our plane pulled away from the gate and started taxiing, the pilot came over the PA system: "Ladies and gentlemen, I'm afraid I've got some more bad news. It's come to my attention that our crew has timed out. We've got to go back to the gate. This flight has been canceled."

I had been at the airport so long, I checked my bag out of desperation—something I don't normally do. All I could think was, "My bag. I need my bag."

I ran off the plane to baggage claim. The handlers looked at each other when I asked them to deliver my suitcase to my hotel, laughing in a way that communicated, *Oh honey, you're not seeing that bag tonight.* My only option was to come back and pick it up tomorrow.

I checked back into the hotel by the office, about 20 minutes from the airport, and climbed into bed naked since I had no clothes with me. I tossed and turned and tossed again—I couldn't sleep because I felt so vulnerable.

Groggy the next morning after having barely slept, I decided to reschedule my flight and go into the office for closing day. It was now Wednesday. We were supposed to have closed the Friday before.

The closing call was set for 2 pm, with Euromoney's London team and our banker, Robert. Fatigued but proud of ourselves for having come through on tying up the equity agreements so quickly, we were stoked for the call.

We were beyond niceties at this point. The Euromoney team just launched right in when we got on the Zoom call.

"One outstanding item..."

Shit.

The issue preventing us from closing five days ago had been our office lease—Euromoney needed paperwork from the landlord, and the leasing company was demanding new paperwork and Euromoney's banking records—all for a $6,000-a-month lease that was going to expire in six months!

Lee and I looked at one another.

"We haven't received that document yet," I volleyed, "but it wasn't required documentation, so—"

The deal guy from Euromoney cut me off. "Yeah, we're thinking we might close this Friday..."

Lee and I exchanged looks again: *What's going on? It's gone from Friday to Wednesday and now Friday again.* It felt like they weren't ready to close the deal on their end and were using the stupid lease as a delay tactic.

Before Lee and I could say anything, Robert broke in, unmuted and raging. "Guys, this is complete bullshit! We've been sitting around with our thumbs up our asses since mid-December. We were supposed to close last Friday. Then it was today. We are not waiting until Friday!"

The Euromoney deal guy was aghast. He sputtered, "I have never been spoken to this way. This is outrageous."

A maddening silence ensued.

I figured this was all part of the game, but Lee and I were shocked—we couldn't believe this was happening.

Then someone said, "Lee and Sharon, what do you think?"

Lee was silent.

I said, "Well, I am disappointed. I thought we were closing Friday. Then I thought we were closing today. I've been in South Carolina for almost two weeks trying to get this done. I need to go home, but I have no idea what to expect in terms of how long this is going to go on. And frankly, I think it's strange that this lease is such a big issue. It's 3,000 square feet in South Carolina—six grand a month, and I personally guarantee it. I mean, we're not talking about the Salesforce tower here."

The Zoom call ended without the deal closing.

Again.

While the Brits were offended by Robert's profanity-laced tirade, they were also upset about what I said and my admittedly snarky tone. Directly after the call, I got an email from Euromoney's deal guy, saying that given some of the comments I made, he was questioning how aligned we were around this deal and requested a meeting between me, Lee and the Euromoney CEO prior to a final signing to make sure we were committed to the positive integration of our team.

Shit. Had I fucked it up? It sounded as if he was threatening to pull the deal. What if they walked away?

The email got Robert even more mad, and I could see that this was not headed in a good direction. I needed to step in and diffuse things, since I'd contributed to the tension now threatening to quash the deal. I told Lee I would take care of it and apologize, though I believed what I'd said was benign. He contributed a great talking point. "If you sensed frustration from me and Lee today, it is coming from a place of disappointment and fatigue. This has been an intense process." It was not a lie.

By now it was Wednesday night. I'd resigned myself to heading home again and would be catching a 10:30 flight Thursday morning. I'd have to get to the airport early to secure a good working space at the Admirals Club for the Zoom meeting with Lee and the CEO from Euromoney. The call was scheduled for 8 am. If all went well, the closing would take place at 9:30—all before my 10:30 flight.

When I got up at 5 am, there was a batch of new emails from our deal team at Leonis. I could see that these guys had barely slept. What a life! I put on my deal suit for the fourth day in a row, including the same underwear. I'd been wearing the suit for days, and it was really uncomfortable, but I didn't have the time to run out and buy sweatpants. It had been a crazy week. We'd been living off fast food because by the time we got out of the office at night, everything else was closed.

I got to the airport by 7 am and set up in a quiet corner of the Admirals Club to take the meeting. Shortly before eight o'clock, the club was overrun with about 20 dudes who were flying off for a ski weekend. They started downing shots and Bloody Marys, getting louder with each round. The CEO was good-natured about it, joking "I guess they're starting their weekend early. You'll be celebrating too, later today!" He advised Lee and me to relax and let the lawyers and bankers do their thing. He knew BI was a great business and was excited about the deal. He said he felt fine about it, and we told him the feeling was mutual.

It was now 9 am, and we were set to close at 9:30. But 9:30 came and went—and no closing call. Lee said things got delayed —to sit tight. Once I was in the air, I kept obsessively checking my phone until I finally decided to leave it alone. Maybe it wasn't happening today—again.

Suddenly my phone pinged: a screenshot of Lee and everyone on the closing call—the bankers, lawyers, buyers, beaming with joy and relief and each giving a thumbs up: the official confirmation that our deal was finally closed. Surrounded by strangers, with no one to talk to or celebrate with, I had no choice but to sit and reflect. I spent the remaining three hours of my flight pondering this momentous event for the first time since I embarked on the process of selling the company. For months, I had been laser-focused on all the little details required to get the deal across the finish line. I had been so consumed by the transaction that I had never paused to consider the greater impact.

What started out as a dream of achieving financial security for my family of four had expanded beyond my wildest dreams, without me even realizing it. Suddenly, it hit me: this was not just about my family. It was about Lee's family. And about all of our employees and their families. And our vendors and their families. We had all done it together, and the ripples of our collective success would be felt far and wide for generations to come. It wasn't just about the money. It was about everyone else who inspired me to pay it forward if I ever had the chance. It was about the kid fresh out of college, discovering he could make a big impact at a small company, and finding his confidence.

When I finally arrived home, I walked into the house, ripped off my stale clothes and dove into the bathtub. At the time, my sister-in-law Lynda was visiting; Lynda, who had inspired me and given me my entrepreneurial start with her vision for Fidget two decades earlier. I came downstairs in a fluffy white robe, my wet hair wrapped in a towel. "Well?" she said. "Shouldn't we have some champagne…or *something*?"

She was right. I scrounged around and found a cheap can of sparkling rose in the back of the fridge. I split it between three champagne glasses and enjoyed a toast with Lynda and Andrew. Finally in the warm embrace of family, I no longer had to hide my exhaustion. I was completely drained.

A little later, I got a FaceTime call from Lee. The way I was looking, I didn't really want to be seen, but I pulled back my wet hair and answered. He was in a bar with some of the OGs and our newer recruits—obviously a few drinks into their celebration.

"Couldn't you have stayed *one* more day?" they bellowed.

I did wish I hadn't left, but it was a joy to see how excited everyone was about what we'd accomplished. We'd done something extraordinary. We'd changed our futures—and we'd done it together, as a team, with hard work, integrity and grit.

Epilogue:
The Next Chapter

Where do I go from here? With the deal closed and our bank accounts enriched by years of hard, bootstrapping work—what comes next? Lee took a break and planned a couple of trips to decompress. Euromoney organized a global meeting to introduce the BI team to their new peers. It had been scheduled for 5 am my time, so I didn't attend, but I heard they showed a collage of everyone at Boardroom Insiders—but pictures of Lee and me weren't included.

I changed my LinkedIn profile and my email address and signature. While Lee was happy to go on his much-deserved vacation, I felt a great sadness. But I didn't feel like I could talk to anyone about it. After all, no one wants to hear a millionaire whine. I only shared my sorrow with my family.

One day, I told Andrew, "Maybe I shouldn't have sold. Maybe this was all a big mistake."

He laughed and said, "Don't be ridiculous. This was your dream. You did it! You did the right thing."

People kept asking me, "What are you going to do now? Aren't you so happy?"

I honestly didn't know how to respond. For weeks, I was in a state of shock.

I live in a neighborhood in San Francisco full of cute shops and restaurants. One weekday shortly after the close, I wandered in and out of shops for a couple of hours. For 20 years, I'd rushed around when I ran errands, purposely avoiding conversations because I felt like I didn't have the time. Now I found myself lingering, and it felt luxurious. I was wearing my red TWA sweatpants and when one shopkeeper asked about them, we had a 15-minute conversation about the new TWA Hotel at JFK Airport. I told him how much he'd love it, and he promised he would go. After I left him, I wandered into a restaurant and had lunch, sipping a glass of rose and catching up on the news on my phone. It felt pretty great, but also strange. I felt aimless.

The new BI leaders told Lee and me that they were coming to South Carolina to meet everyone—that we'd have a nice dinner together to celebrate. We'd only seen these people on Zoom calls, and I was looking forward to meeting them, so I kept waiting for the call—excited I would get to go back one more time.

But the call never came.

I was still corresponding with the CEO periodically to tie up loose ends, and at one point I offered to have Lee and me join in when they met the team, but he politely skirted the issue.

When Lee returned from vacation, I told him I didn't think we were going to be invited when they came to visit.

"Nah," he said, "I'm sure they're planning to include us."

"No, they're not, Lee."

A couple of weeks earlier, when I'd been talking with Euromoney's HR person, she likened our work culture to a cult of personality. That's when I realized they just wanted us out of the way. We were like mom and dad—our employees would jokingly call us that. Euromoney thought it best to have the teams break ties with us as quickly as possible. And in retrospect, I think that was the right move.

I knew I was taking it too personally, but that didn't help—I felt like I'd lost my brood. I hoped that being part of a multinational company would give everybody the opportunity to take new career paths. Lee and I had always been challenged to help successful, ambitious people grow because we were a small company and didn't always have a place for them to advance.

After weeks of not knowing what to do with myself, I started putting some TLC into my home—which had been long neglected, battered by kids and pets. It made it easier to put it all in my rearview mirror. I've always been comfortable with change, often making arbitrary choices about what to do next with my life. While I know a lot more about how the world works and what makes me tick, I'm still making decisions by intuition. But, considering where it got me, I'm thinking maybe it's time to trust myself.

Sharing my knowledge and experience with others like me, trying to realize their entrepreneurial dreams, is becoming my singular focus. What I can bring to the entrepreneurial landscape is humanity, model leadership and mentorship—and to help make entrepreneurship accessible to everyone, regardless of their background. I'm now a limited partner in a women-run venture fund that supports female-founded startups. Their portfolio companies are doing astonishing things, such as making artificial scallops and chicken out of air protein, testing wastewater to detect community spread of disease, and plant-based synthetic breast milk. I've attended female-focused business events, meeting young women who are real badasses. Most are younger than I was when I started Fidget, and they're confident and unafraid.

I also attend a monthly meetup of women business leaders. Some succeed by climbing the corporate ladder, while others are entrepreneurs like me. A few of us followed the same path— we saw a little opening to create something that serves a need not being met.

And I still track the C-suite. Women now make up 20 percent of the CIOs of Fortune 500 companies, and more than 10 percent of the Fortune 500 are led by women CEOs. That might not sound like much, but it's progress. The likelihood of entrepreneurial success remains low for women, but the landscape is slowly changing for the better.

I believe we can make our mark with integrity and humanity —the way Lee and I did at Boardroom Insiders. For years, industry experts, potential partners and funders sounded the alarm about how much our business model relied on people. But in the end, it was our team who propelled us forward. No matter how far the industry pivots to artificial intelligence and pays tribute to the almighty dollar, people are still the foundation for success. How can we lift each other up? How do we foster employees and empower leaders who go on to build their own capable, righteous teams?

This will be our legacy.

Scan for more information and tools on
how to become a successful entrepreneur and
plan a successful company exit:

www.sharonkgillenwater.com

PROLOGUE: THE PAYOFF

1. Hinchliffe, E. (2023, June 5). *Women CEOs run 10.4% of fortune 500 companies. A quarter of the 52 leaders became CEO in the last year.* Fortune. https://fortune.com/2023/06/05/fortune-500-companies-2023-women-10-percent/.
2. Kersten, A., & Athanasia, G. (2022, October 20). *Addressing the gender imbalance in venture capital and entrepreneurship.* CSIS. https://www.csis.org/analysis/addressing-gender-imbalance-venture-capital-and-entrepreneurship.
3. US VC female founders Dashboard - Pitchbook. Accessed January 30, 2024. https://pitchbook.com/news/articles/the-vc-female-founders-dashboard.
4. Taylor, Harriet. "Amid Economic Uncertainty, Women Make Fortune 500 C-Suite Progress, but See Startup Funding Plateau." CNBC, January 2, 2024. https://www.cnbc.com/2023/12/28/amid-2023-economic-uncertainty-women-make-c-suite-progress-see-vc-funding-plateau.html.
5. Zimmerman, Eilene. "Only 2% of Women-Owned Businesses Break the $1 Million Mark -- Here's How to Be One of Them." Forbes, July 1, 2015. https://www.forbes.com/sites/eilenezimmerman/2015/04/01/only-2-of-women-owned-businesses-break-the-1-million-mark-heres-how-to-be-one-of-them/?sh=7272a85d27a6.

1. BLUE COLLAR WITH A TWIST

1. Little, J. (2022, November 24). *Residents revel after Starbucks gives up on Ocean Beach.* NBC 7 San Diego. https://www.nbcsandiego.com/news/local/residents-revel-after-starbucks-gives-up-on-ocean-beach/3105691/.

Acknowledgments

TO MY COLLABORATORS

I am grateful to Michael Ahn for encouraging me to start a new career as an author and speaker. Back in June 2021, we sat in my living room until 2am drinking bourbon and sharing stories. It was Michael who convinced me to tell mine. He interviewed me for hours and pulled together the first draft of this book, which sat on the shelf for two years as it was rejected by every single publisher and agent because I "didn't have a platform." Then, in October 2023, I spoke with Elizabeth Pearson. She told me to get on TikTok, pursue a hybrid publishing deal with Legacy Launch Pad and own 100 percent of my book because "you'll never go wrong betting on yourself." I followed her instructions precisely. I am grateful to Elizabeth for her advice, and also to the Legacy Launch Pad team, especially Crystal Sershen and Ryan Aliapoulios, who made my manuscript sing.

TO MY MENTORS

My circuitous career path led me to mentors who changed my life in profound ways and contributed to my success. The encouragement that Ginny Butterfield and Maribeth Mellin provided at my first "real" job at *San Diego Magazine* made me feel worthy and confident in a professional setting. They also showed me what a workplace can be when women are in charge. Tricia Roth did the same when she hired me as a sales-person at DLC. Her dedication to customers shaped my convictions about how they should be treated, which became a touchstone of Boardroom Insiders' culture. Paolo Zeppa introduced me to tech marketing, taught me the ropes and pulled me along as he rose through the ranks. This lucrative and rewarding new career allowed me to sustain my family as I piloted and built Boardroom Insiders.

Cindy Wilson gave me my first opportunity to explore the concept and methodology that became Boardroom Insiders. Ben Phillipps pulled back the curtain to the C-suite and helped me understand what CXOs value and trust and how they make decisions. And Mary Fehrnstrom, perhaps the single biggest champion of Boardroom Insiders, helped me pilot, validate and refine my frameworks and methodologies for well over a decade, leading to the design and launch of BI Pro, our game-changing software.

TO MY ADVISORS AND MONEY MEN

When people ask me what to look for in an angel investor, I tell them three things: only take money from people who aren't going to need or miss it; make sure they are seasoned entrepreneurs so they understand what you are going through; and look for people who will give you advice—when you ask for it. I was blessed to have three such people on my side.

Michael Blend may have no idea how much his $125K check back in 2008 motivated me to keep going during tough times. His investment made Boardroom Insiders real and ignited a single-minded determination in me that burned hot for 14 years until the day we sold the company. In short, there was no way in hell I was going to lose his fucking money! Michael was also a critical advisor, particularly during the M&A process. Bobby Martin and Wil Brawley also inspired, advised and invested in our vision, and Bobby checked in with me regularly in those precarious early days and introduced me to my business partner Lee, who changed everything for the better.

TO MY FELLOW TRAVELERS AND VENDORS

When you run a company, vendors of every stripe try to pass themselves off as your "partners," but few are worthy of the label. Two of Boardroom Insiders' vendors were partners in the truest sense of the word. Our companies "grew up" together, and we became entrepreneurial confidants. We were the first customer for Matt Manning's company, Information Evolution, and we had a wonderful dedicated team there, most of whom still work for Boardroom Insiders. We also gave Dualboot Partners their very first project in 2018. I was inspired by our first meeting with Todd Buelow, Ben Gilman and Daniel DelaCruz in our little office in Fort Mill, South Carolina. I knew then that we had finally found the technology partner we needed to deliver on our product vision. As these two great companies continue to grow and thrive, I will be cheering them on!

TO MY PARTNER AND TEAM

There would be no story of Boardroom Insiders without Lee Demby. Lee brought an incredible toolbox of experience, talents and dedication to our business. And for everything else, there was always "someone in his neighborhood," which is how we connected with so many vendors, contractors and employees over the years. I couldn't have asked for a better or more capable partner and I will be forever grateful to him and his family for coming on this journey with me. Lee also brought Melanie Strain on board, who was and continues to be a secret weapon at Boardroom Insiders. Working with Melanie and watching her grow into a respected and empathetic developer of young talent was one of the highlights of my career. I also have tremendous gratitude and respect for our "OGs" (you know who you are) and the entire Boardroom Insiders team. We had a great thing going, and I miss you all.

TO MY FRIENDS AND FAMILY

For 14 years, I had a single-minded obsession with Boardroom Insiders that probably made me a habitual bore at social gatherings, if I even attended at all. Thank you to my friends and family for putting up with it. I even occasionally pulled them into my Boardroom Insiders world, recruiting them to work on various projects for the company. This includes but is not limited to: Tali, Chris, LindaKay, Mike, Carlos, Felix, Andrew, Cousin Matt, TK, Doug, Mary, Caron and others.

As for family, I am in awe of my husband Andrew's unwavering support and love. He believed in me more than I believed in myself and talked me off a ledge on the regular, usually in the middle of the night. My boys, who had no choice in the matter, were also along for the ride. As a momtrepreneur, I was present but mostly distracted, head down in a laptop during nights, weekends and family vacations. As I watch them begin their own careers, I see the upside of their upbringing in their natural business acumen, curiosity, independence and drive. I founded and built a company to have a rewarding career and achieve financial independence, but seeing a positive impact of my work in the next generation is the best reward.

About the Author

Sharon K. Gillenwater is a SaaS start-up adviser, Inc. 5000 entrepreneur, speaker and author. She is the co-founder of Fidget.com and Boardroom Insiders, where she served as CEO. In 2022, Boardroom Insiders was acquired by Euromoney LLC, leading Gillenwater to a $25M exit. Gillenwater lives in the San Francisco Bay Area. *Scaling with Soul* is her first book.

Photo by Andrew Keeler

Printed in the USA
CPSIA information can be obtained
at www.ICGtesting.com
CBHW031048030624
9307CB00003B/24